Henry Owen, Henry Butts Owen

**Sixteen Sermons on Various Subjects**

Henry Owen, Henry Butts Owen
**Sixteen Sermons on Various Subjects**
ISBN/EAN: 9783743349339
Manufactured in Europe, USA, Canada, Australia, Japa
Cover: Foto ©Lupo / pixelio.de

Manufactured and distributed by brebook publishing software (www.brebook.com)

Henry Owen, Henry Butts Owen

**Sixteen Sermons on Various Subjects**

# SIXTEEN
# SERMONS

ON

# VARIOUS SUBJECTS.

BY

THE REV. DR. HENRY OWEN,

LATE RECTOR OF ST. OLAVE, HART-STREET,

AND

MANY YEARS VICAR OF EDMONTON, MIDDLESEX.

LONDON.

Printed for J. NICHOLS, Red-Lion-Passage, Fleet Street;
and F. and C. RIVINGTON, St. Paul's Church Yard.
Sold also by Mr. BLISS, Oxford; Mr. DEIGHTON, Cambridge;
and Mr. BARRET, Bond Street, Bath.
1797.

# ADVERTISEMENT.

THE following Sermons were compofed for the particular edification of three congregations, confifting of perfons in the middle and lower ranks of life; without the moft diftant idea of their ever being fubmitted to general criticifm.

They

They are now reluctantly produced to the world, not for the credit of the writer, but for the benefit of his *five* unprovided daughters.

The Author's reputation ſtands on a much firmer baſis: a long life uniformly devoted to the intereſts of ſacred learning, and the advancement of Chriſtian virtue.

The Editor truſts that he may ſafely rely on the candor of the Public for thoſe proper allowances which a poſthumous Publication, under the above-ſtated circumſtances, ſeems to claim: not doubting but that it will readily extend

## ADVERTISEMENT.  vii

extend that liberality to the *perform-ance* which it has so eminently shewn to the *family* of a man, who, in all his labors, whether from the pulpit or the press, conscientiously endeavoured to improve his fellow-creatures, rather than to display his own abilities.

The Editor has only to add, that the gratitude of the Author's Family is as sincere as the benevolence of the Public has been great.

Edmonton,
Feb. 16, 1797.            H. B. O.

# SERMON I.

# SERMON I.

ROMANS ii.—Ver. 28, 29.

FOR HE IS NOT A JEW, WHO IS ONE OUTWARDLY; NEITHER IS THAT CIRCUMCISION, WHICH IS OUTWARD IN THE FLESH:

BUT HE IS A JEW, WHO IS ONE INWARDLY; AND CIRCUMCISION IS THAT OF THE HEART, IN THE SPIRIT, AND NOT IN THE LETTER, WHOSE PRAISE IS NOT OF MEN, BUT OF GOD.

St. Paul, in the beginning of this Epiftle, defcribes the wretched and deplorable ftate, into which Mankind were univerfally fallen;—and thence infers the great ne-

neceffity of fome new difpenfation, to bring them to the practice of virtue and holinefs, in order to regain the favour of God.

He begins his account with the character of the Gentiles.—And thefe he fhews, from a particular enumeration of their feveral vices, to be fo depraved both in mind and morals, as, without the intervention of faith and repentance, to be in the utmoft danger of perifhing for ever.

The Jews were poffeffed of greater advantages; and thought themfelves confequently in a fafer condition. They were in covenant with God; and had his law in their hands to direct their conduct. But this law, which they fo much gloried in, had no influence on their hearts and lives. Their practices daily contradicted their profeffion; and, inftead of doing honour to the name of God, brought it into contempt even among the Heathens. Thus they perverted the means of goodnefs into an occafion of more aggravated guilt; and by that abufe rendered themfelves obnoxious to much greater punifhments, than thofe who offended againft a lefs perfect law.

But they deluded themfelves into a fatal fecurity; and thought it impoffible they could ever mifcarry while they enjoyed the benefit of circumcifion, which entitled them to the privileges of the covenant. To free them therefore from the power of this deceit, the Apoftle acquaints them, that " their circumcifion would indeed " profit them if they lived in ftrict obe- " dience to the law; and faithfully per- " formed the terms of the covenant;—but " if they became tranfgreffors of the " law,

"law, and indulged themselves in vice
"and immorality; their circumcision
"would be so far from conveying any
"right or benefit to them, that they might
"as well not have been circumcised at
"all." Nay, he assures them, that "the
"Heathens themselves, if they led better
"lives than the Jews—if they were more
"observant of the law of Nature, than
"the others were of the law of Moses—
"that these Heathens, I say, though they
"had no circumcision in their flesh, were
"more truly the children of Abraham;
"and more entitled to the promises of
"God; than any of the carnal Jews, who
"had the mark of circumcision upon
"them." For, as he concludes in the
words of my text, "He is not a Jew,
"who is one outwardly; neither is that
"circumcision, which is outward in the
"flesh; but he is a Jew, who is one in-
"wardly;

" wardly; and circumcifion is that of the
" the heart, in the fpirit, and not in the
" letter, whofe praife is not of men, but
" of GOD." As if he had faid, Every one
that is born a Jew, and can plead his admiffion into the covenant of GOD, is not
therefore the real and proper Jew, to
whom the benefits of the covenant belong; nor is that the true available circumcifion, which is outwardly apparent
in the flefh; but he is the Jew, the Ifraelite indeed, who, in the integrity of his
heart, yields obedience to the divine laws,
and walks worthy of thofe high privileges,
which GOD has conferred upon him; and
the true acceptable circumcifion is that of
him, who cuts off the fuperfluities of
naughtinefs, and the impurities of fin;
—who hath the law of righteoufnefs,
of which circumcifion is the fign, imprinted on his inner man, on his Soul

and spirit,—and who therefore makes it the great business of his life to approve himself to God by a diligent discharge of his various duties.

These are the remonstrances which the Apostle thought fit to make to the *Jews*. But what are these remonstrances, you'll say, to us *Christians*? Why, truly, they are important lessons—such as we may greatly profit by, if we are not wanting to our own improvement. For, only change the terms—put the word Christian instead of Jew, and Baptism in the place of Circumcision, and the text assumes a modern form—exactly fits the present times—and comes home with full weight into our own bosoms.

Mankind have been always prone to impose upon themselves in religious matters

## SERMON I.

ters by vain and empty delusions. And, if we compare these delusions together, we shall find, that, in all Ages, and among all nations, they have been very similar to each other. This may be proved by various instances in the conduct of Jews and Christians; who, though they differ in *other* respects, are yet in *this* unhappily uniform.

If the Jews relied on their Descent from Abraham—trusted to their being circumcised, and having the true Religion of GOD among them: if they placed their confidence in these outward advantages, and hoped to be saved at last, let them lead what kind of life they would: how many Christians are there, who support themselves, and build their hopes of GOD's favour, on the same or as weak a foundation? who trust to their being baptized in the

name

name of Chrift, and to their profeffing his Religion, for all the promifes that he hath made to the faithful? But, pray, where is the difference (I fpeak with regard to real merit) between being natural-born Jews, and being born of Chriftian parents? between an outward Circumcifion, and an outward Baptifm? between an external Profeffion of the Law of Mofes, and an external Profeffion of the Gofpel of Chrift? If we blame the Jews for their foolifh notions, how can we poffibly exculpate ourfelves? If we think *their* Privileges to be of no value without the addition of a holy Life; then what can *our* Privileges avail us, unlefs we live anfwerably to them? They are indeed of great ufe, as means and inftruments of virtue; but if we do not make that ufe of them, they only ferve to increafe our condemnation.

tion. Baptifm and the other **Ordinances** of Religion were not eftablifhed for their own fake; but for further and nobler **Ends**: that we might be obliged and enabled thereby to follow the example of our Saviour Chrift; and live up to the Precepts he has given us. And wo be to us, if they have not at laft this effect upon us!

Again: if the Jews depended on the profeffion of Religion, and refted for Salvation on their Knowledge of the Law; how many Chriftians are there among us, who turn the Gofpel into mere fpeculation, and judge of the proficiency they have made under it by the foundnefs of their Faith, and the orthodoxy of their Opinions? who are for ever adjufting what they fhould believe; and never trouble themfelves with what they fhould *practife?* But is not this a very a very wrong reprefentation of Chriftianity? For though we *know* the things of it ever fo well, yet our Saviour affures us, we are then only in the way to be happy, when we are fo wife as to *do* them. Whatever knowledge of Chrift and his Religion any of us may pretend to, ftill it behoves us to remember, that " hereby alone we can be fure that we know him, if we keep his Commandments. And he that faith, He knoweth him, and keepeth not his commandments, is as void of truth, as he is of morality." He deceives himfelf, and will be finally wretched.

Moreover, if the Jews expreffed greater zeal for the rituals and ceremonials, than for the moral duties of the law; if they were more exact in performing the outward and fhadowy part of their Religion, than in cultivating inward and fubftantial

Ho-

Holiness; how many Christians are there, who are deeply tinctured with the same principles; and run after them into the like practices? who are very scrupulous in the observance of *some* religious acts, and intolerably negligent in the practice of *others?* How many persons are there in the world, who continually pray for grace to amend, and yet never exert the least care to suppress their sinful and vicious inclinations? How many do we see, who are strict, perhaps, in keeping the Sabbath, and every day of the week after make shipwreck of their faith, and a good conscience? Nay, how many are there who approach the altar, and solemnly vow obedience to the Almighty; and yet instantly return to the commission of those sins, which just before they had promised to renounce?

But

But in vain do they thus worship God. To render thefe outward fervices acceptable, they fhould add to them the inward devotion of their fouls. True religion is a vital principle, regulating the whole conduct of life. It makes a man a new creature; and fubdues every thing in him, that exalts itfelf againft the difcipline of Christ. He who is truly actuated by it; is fo far from refting in the outward privileges he enjoys; that he makes thofe very privileges an argument to himfelf, for working out his falvation with more fear and trembling—well knowing, that the greater his *advantages* are, the greater his obligations to improve by them.

Accordingly, he watches every opportunity, and lays hold of every incidence, that opens the way to a good action. He endeavours to yield an univerfal obedience to to the laws of God. He never overvalues some kind of duties to the disparagement of others; but gives *every* duty its due place in his esteem; and is ready to shew the sincerity of his regard, by complying with it as occasion requires. In all this, however, he has no view to the praise of men, but only to the approbation of God. It is the conscience of his duty that is the great spring of all his actions;—and therefore he is always consistent—always like himself;—as religious and devout in private, as he is in public;—as careful of himself and his proceedings when nobody sees him, as when the eyes of the world are fixed upon him. Yet, he is far from assuming on this account. What he has been enabled to do he ascribes entirely to the goodness of God; and humbly applies it to his glory. He is still in his own apprehension an unprofitable servant; he

has

has done his benefactor no good—" he "has only done what he ought to do;" and therefore pleads no merit. But with God he knows there is mercy; and as he has *already* derived from his grace the power of serving him in the manner he has done; so he hopes to receive, from the same grace, in futurity, the reward of those imperfect, but well-meant services.,

These are the genuine marks of Christianity: And he that has these characters upon him, is a real and sincere Christian:—one that is now in the favour of God; and shall hereafter enjoy the promises of the Gospel. No other pretences, no privileges, no endowments, will ever stand us in any stead. For they are not the hearers of the Law, or the professors of the Gospel, but the doers and observers of it, that shall be justified. Therefore, we must suffer

suffer our Religion to sink deep into our hearts; and to produce the fruits of righteousness in our lives; if we mean to be the better; nay, if we mean not to be the worse, for the profession of it. We must carefully apply it—to the government of our passions—to the improvement of our dispositions—and to the reformation of our lives and manners. If it can become us to suppose any one time fitter than another for taking such pains with ourselves; when, I beseech you, can the good work be more seasonably undertaken, than at this very time? The time that opens a new scene of life, by introducing us into a new year. And may the new year, we are now commencing, effectually inspire us with new resolutions of employing it better than we have done the last! When this is sincerely determined upon, and we live like those who must give an account,

C then

then these additions or lengthenings of life become a matter of real joy. For, the the more service we pay, the greater reward we shall be sure to receive. But let us in no wise deceive ourselves by false calculations; and, because the *Sun* is returned to the same point of the Heavens that he was in a year ago; imagine ourselves to be also in the same situation, and the same state of life. In truth, our circumstances are now very different from what they were a year ago. The state of our accounts is greatly altered; and the time when we shall be called to deliver them up, is so much the nearer to us. How many have been called upon already, within the compass of this last revolution, who promised to themselves as long a continuance, as any of us can reasonably do? Think then of their fate: and let that thought instruct you—whether you ought

## SERMON I.

in prudence to rely on finishing the course of *this* year, which you are now entering :—And whether you ought not *so* to begin it, as to resolve that it shall be a new year to you, in the most christian and beneficial sense. This we certainly owe to the distinguishing providence of GOD, whose goodness in our preservation calls for the thanks of living to his glory. This we certainly owe to ourselves, whose happiness depends upon well-doing; and whose time otherwise employed, serves only to increase the miseries of eternity.

Let the time past of our lives therefore suffice us to have wrought the will of the Gentiles; and to have indulged the sensual inclinations of our hearts. And let us so number the days that are yet to come, as to apply our thoughts unto true wisdom;

dom;—to that wisdom which is from above, and which seeks the things that are above. Things that will endure, when weeks, months, and years shall be no more; but things that are fitted to make us happy, who shall likewise survive the ruins of time. To the enjoyment of which things—even a glorious inheritance reserved in Heaven for us. GOD, of his infinite mercy, bring us all, through JESUS CHRIST our LORD, to whom with the FATHER, and the HOLY GHOST, be ascribed all honour, &c. Amen.

# SERMON II.

# SERMON II.

LUKE xvii.—Ver. 21.

BEHOLD, THE KINGDOM OF GOD IS WITHIN YOU.

IT is manifestly of the utmost importance, that every Christian be well instructed, and firmly settled in the Faith: that he be fully persuaded, and thoroughly convinced, by good arguments, of the truth and Authority of the Gospel. And good arguments indeed there are, drawn both

## SERMON. II.

from its *internal* and *external* character which prove it to be truly derived from GOD. Of all the various proofs that might be urged, I shall at present insist only on one; but that such an one as every Man, who impartially consults the dictates of his own heart, must acknowledge at once to be sufficiently plain, and at the same time sufficiently conclusive.

We have been, somehow, so much accustomed to seek *abroad*, in *outward* testimonies, for the proofs and evidences of Christianity, that we have never properly attended to that strongest proof of all, which exists at *home*, in our *inward* perceptions. The text is adapted to correct this mistake; and to put us upon a right inquiry. It assures us, that " the Kingdom of God," or, as I consider it, " the Truth of the Gospel," is to be discovered " within in us." And this difcovery it exhorts us alfo to " behold"—to obferve and take notice of; as a thing that is of infinite weight and moment: conducive to our happinefs in feveral refpects.

But before I come to difcufs this point, it may be of ufe to obferve, that the doctrine of the text is founded on a certain maxim, fo plain and perfpicuous in itfelf, as to be here taken for granted. The maxim I mean is this.—" That the perceptions of human nature are exactly correfpondent with the declarations of fcripture: and that confequently they bear mutual teftimony to each other." And who, that examines the contents of the Gofpel, and compares them with the fentiments of his own mind, can ever doubt the truth of this maxim? When we make the comparifon, it obtrudes itfelf upon us; and forces

us

us to acknowledge its truth and reality. No echo can anfwer more clearly to the voice that raifes it, than the fentiments of our hearts anfwer to what the Gofpel preaches to us. And this I fhall now endeavour to fhew to be the fhorteft and fureft of all methods to difcover and afcertain the truth of the Gofpel.

The *two* principal doctrines of the Gofpel are thofe which relate to our *Fall*, and our *Redemption*. By the doctrine of the *Fall* we are reprefented as depraved and finful creatures; ftrangely difordered in our faculties and affections; miferably alienated from God and goodnefs; and perverfely inclined to vice and immorality.

Need we any book, but the book of our own hearts; need we any teftimony, but the teftimony of our own confciences, to be convinced of the truth of this doctrine? When

## SERMON II.

When we look into ourselves, and calmly attend to what passes within us; do we not find, do we not *feel*, that we are all great and grievous sinners, hurried on by unruly passions, and betrayed into ruin by corrupt appetites? And what now is the language of this sad disorder we **feel** within: Does it not plainly tell us, not in the sound of words, but by the less ambiguous voice of Nature, that we are all *fallen* creatures :—sunk far below that upright state, in which a good and gracious God must have originally created us?

And yet, even in this sinful, disordered state, have we not a certain dislike to our vices—a certain abhorrence of wicked actions? Nay, have we not innate love for virtue and goodness—a lively sense of their being proper for us? Are we not ashamed, when we act unworthy of ourselves—and glad, when

when we appear to have good qualities? What then is this contrariety we feel—this pronenefs to ill, and this ftruggle againft it? What is it! but the voice of our Nature proclaiming again, in the moft expreffive manner, that we are *redeemed* creatures: " that there is in us an inward " Redeemer, a light of the mind, a feed " of goodnefs, an inftinct to virtue—mer- " cifully given us by our heavenly Father " upon the fall, to be the foundation of " our future recovery."

What then does the Gofpel fay to us of the fall of man, that our hearts do not alfo fay? Or what does it fay to us of our redemption, that is not alfo faid to us by the ftate of our own fouls? For, if we were not fallen, how could we labour under fo much corruption? And if we were not redeemed, how could we feel a diflike
of

of sin? How could we obtain an inclination to goodnefs, and a defire of appearing virtuous?—For, what elfe is this defire of goodnefs, but a certain inward principle that has begun our redemption, and is labouring to carry it on?

To render this labour effectual is the whole defign of the Chriftian religion. All its doctrines, all its precepts, and all its inftitutions, have an immediate relation, and direct tendency, to this end—a direct tendency to fupprefs and eradicate the *evil* of our nature, and to ftrengthen and improve the *good* that is in us, till it finally become *triumphant.*

The truth of this will evidently appear by a brief confideration of particulars.

Of the two pofitive *inftitutions* of Religion, the *firft*, that is, *Baptifm,* admits us into

into the Christian church; and endows us with such means, as may enable us to correct our original depravity; and to go on advancing in virtue and goodness.

And if, in consequence of the privileges which Baptism confers upon us, we are careful to perform the obligations of it, we shall perceive our nature continually growing more improved; and our good dispositions becoming of course more strengthened and confirmed.

But since the very best of us, in this frail state, cannot with all our care, keep ourselves clear of all offences; therefore the *other* institution, the *Sacrament* of the Lord's *Supper*, was appointed and ordained as the means of reconciling us again, on our sincere repentance, to our offended Father; and of obtaining from him farther

ther supplies of his heavenly grace, to invigorate our powers for better services. And when we duly and devoutly partake of this Sacrament, do we not find our dispositions meliorated—our love of GOD and goodness increased—and ourselves, in consequence, carried on with more ardent zeal towards every thing virtuous and praise-worthy?

How suitable then are these *institutions* to the frame of our nature, and the exigencies of our condition? And who could apply them with such effect to the benefit and improvement of man, but " *He* who " knew what was in Man," and by what means he was to be raised and perfected?

To help us forwards in the way of perfection, the *precepts* of the Gospel come next to our assistance, and offer themselves

as

as our guides. Thofe which are *negative*, forbidding evil, plainly fhew us all the vices we fhould ftrive to avoid; and thofe which are *affirmative*, directing to good, point out to us the virtues we fhould labour to attain.

If we compare thefe *precepts* with the dictates of our *moral fenfe*, how conformable are they to each other? and how juft it is to conclude, that He who planted in us that moral fenfe muft be likewife the author of thofe moral precepts.

The fentiments of Human Nature and the precepts of religion fpeak exactly the fame language; and both, the language of God. For what does the Gofpel forbid, but what reafon tells us is wrong to be done? Or, what does the Gofpel enjoin, but what reafon always recommends

to

## SERMON II.

to our practice? And when we strictly follow these Gospel rules—when we are studious to avoid evil, and zealous in the performance of good works, do we not find ourselves improved accordingly, and dignified by the approbation of our own minds?

But these *precepts*, however reasonable, are not of themselves always sufficient to engage and secure our observance: they stand in need of *proper sanctions*, to give them weight, force, and authority. Such sanctions therefore the *declarations* of the Gospel exhibit to us—by shewing us the happy or miserable consequences, that respectively attend our good or evil actions, through the course of time, and through the ages of eternity. And these consequences we may observe, though they seem to flow from the constitution of Nature,

ture, are yet always set before us, either by way of *rewards* proposed, or *punishments* denounced, rather than as simple *predictions*, that they might sink deeper into our minds, and have more influence on our practice.

With respect to *this* world, the Scripture expresly affirms, that " peace and " happiness will be our certain lot, as " long as we are followers of that which " is good;" but, if we deviate into the paths of wickedness, the same Scripture positively declares that " pain and sor-" row, distress and anguish, misery and " unhappiness, will, sooner or later, be " sure to overtake us." And does not the constitution of Nature, and our own experience of its operations, vouch for the truth of this declaration? A declaration that could be ascertained by none, but by Him alone who created man; and who,

from

from the beginning determined, how differently he should be affected in different circumstances.

These different affections we accordingly feel. We have always in our minds a sense of happiness when we act aright; and a sense of misery when we behave wickedly. And these different sensations, were we to continue for ever in this world, would also for ever attend us, according to our different conduct. And since *this* world and the *next* are confessedly but two parts of one uniform moral system, does not reason strongly suggest, that those actions, habits, and dispositions, which contributed to our happiness or misery in the present life, will necessarily be attended with similar effects in the life which is to come? and that we shall therefore be *eternally* wretched or otherwife, as we have been *temporally* good or bad?

Now, what Reafon fuggefts, the Gofpel confirms. For, it plainly afferts, that in a *future* ftate, " every one will be fen-
" tenced to receive the things done in his
" body, according to that he hath done,
" whether it be good or evil;" and that, in confequence of this fentence, " the
" wicked fhall go away into everlafting
" punifhment, but the righteous into life
" eternal."

Thefe are the fanctions that urge our obfervance of the divine laws: and if thefe fanctions fail of their effect, nothing further remains to be offered. For, higher motives cannot be propofed to the underftanding of man, than thofe which refult from the awful confideration of endlefs
tor-

torments and of life eternal —Here therefore *revelation* clofes; and leaves us to make our choice.

Now, whilft we have it in our power to choofe, we cannot furely but choofe *life*. But, if we are earneft in this choice, let us be careful to remember, that " if we " would enter into life, we muft keep the " commandments"—muft obferve and obey the rules of the Gofpel: rules, which our SAVIOUR has kindly given us for our guidance and direction—rules, which He has gracioufly exemplified for our ufe and encouragement.

But to become, as we ought, truly obfervant of thefe rules, and faithful to the calls of duty, we muft previoufly be endowed with a love to GOD, and a liking to virtue and goodnefs. For we can never

ha-

habitually act well, unless we are habitually well disposed. Now, to improve in us these necessary good dispositions—to inspire our hearts with divine love; to incline our affections to true piety; and to quicken our power in the exercise of it; is the great end, as I have already observed, and the sole aim of those religious services, which the Gospel so strenuously recommends to our own use. For those services were purposely established, " that " we might profit thereby." And admirably are they adapted, if duly performed, to become profitable to us:—to be the means of making us " holy, harmless, undefiled, separate from sinners, and at last partakers of the kingdom of Heaven."

As therefore we value these virtuous endowments, and wish to attain these heavenly blessings, let us always be careful

to

## SERMON II.

to " give diligent attendance, to reading," to inſtruction, to prayer, to meditation; and all the ordinances of Religion; more eſpecially to the devout celebration of the holy *Sacrament*—that moſt exalted, moſt divine, moſt heart-enlivening portion of all Chriſtan worſhip.

To neglect, as is cuſtomary with too many—to neglect theſe ſacred ordinances, is, alas! to neglect our own good. It is, oh dreadful conſideration! it is, to deprive ourſelves of " the means of grace," and to extinguiſh in ourſelves " the hope " of glory."—For what hope can we have of attaining at laſt " the end of our cal- " ling; the ſalvation of our ſouls;" if we preſumptuouſly deſpiſe thoſe very means, which God has appointed for the attainment of it? He, who created us in a ſtate of innocence, and who had compaſsion upon us when we corrupted ourselves, best knew the method that would insure our recovery. That method is comprised in the established ordinances of Religion. Which ordinances, faithfully observed, will enable us, partly by their natural fitness, and partly by supernatural grace annexed, to correct the perverseness of our evil dispositions, and to improve in the virtues of a holy life.

If the world and its temptations should assault our integrity, and labour to seduce us from the right path; let us look forward to the issue of things—to those eternal rewards and punishments, that finally await us in another state. They are more than sufficient to outweigh all other considerations. For what has the world to offer, either in terrours or in allurements, that is worthy to be compared

with

with those joys and torments; which heaven and hell present to our view? And what folly is it, to be influenced by the light, the transient occurences of time, in preference to the momentous, the everlasting concerns of eternity?

The sum of the whole is this—We have a revealed religion proposed for our acceptance, to whose truth and divine authority our own hearts and consciences bear ample testimony. The great design of this religion is, to correct what is wrong, and to improve what is right, in our nature: its great design is, to make us virtuous and holy in this life, that we may be eternally happy in the other. With this view it lays before us just and perfect rules of conduct; which it enjoins us carefully to observe. To dispose us the better to observe them, it prescribes to our use certain

tain ordinances, adapted to fupprefs our carnal inclinations, and to raife our affections to fpiritual things. And to engage us the more firmly to cultivate in ourfelves thefe good difpofitions, as well as to practife the duties of our ftations, it opens a profpect into the other world, and fets before us the glorious rewards annexed to virtue, and the dreadful punifhments adjudged to vice: rewards and punifhments that will laft for ever.

Having then, my dearly beloved, fuch view of things before our eyes; having fuch promifes of happinefs on the one hand, and fuch denunciations of mifery on the other; how much does it concern us, in point of wifdom, in point of duty, in point of intereft, to attend diligently to the voice of Religion! and, in obedience to its
precepts

precepts, to cleanſe ourſelves from all filthineſs of fleſh and ſpirit—from all impurities of life, and from every ſenſual affection, " perfecting holineſs in the fear of God!"

SERMON

# SERMON III.

# SERMON III.

### MATTHEW xi.—2, 3.

NOW WHEN JOHN HAD HEARD IN THE PRISON THE WORKS OF CHRIST, HE SENT TWO OF HIS DISCIPLES, AND SAID UNTO HIM, ART THOU HE THAT SHOULD COME, OR DO WE LOOK FOR ANOTHER?

MY intention, in this discourse, is not to inculcate any particular doctrine; but to explain to you at large that portion of Scripture, which was just now read for the Gospel of the day; a portion of Scripture that justly merits a very full and critical

tical examination; as it has been often varioufly, but moft egregioufly ill-interpreted, not only to the detriment of the fenfe, but alfo to the difparagement of the Baptift's character.

From the queftion here propofed—Art thou he that fhould come, or do we look for another?—fome of our commentators have inferred, that JOHN the BAPTIST, at this time, greatly doubted whether JESUS was indeed the promifed MESSIAH; an inference in no wife countenanced by the text. For furely He, who bore fuch ample and repeated teftimonies to the bleffed JESUS—who *faw* the Spirit defcending upon him—who *heard* him proclaimed from Heaven the Son of GOD—who himfelf *pointed* to him as the lamb of GOD that taketh away the fins of the world—and who earneftly *exhorted* all the people to believe

lieve in him, and to obey him: He, I fay, who, through the courfe of his miniftry, made fuch open and folemn declarations in favour of CHRIST, can never be fuppofed to *doubt* at laft, of his being the perfon that was to come,—that is, the long expected MESSIAH.

Hence then, others have concluded, that the Baptift did not fend this meffage on his own account, but purely for the fake and conviction of his difciples:—with a view to fet *them* right in their notions; and to confirm them in the belief of JESUS being the true MESSIAH. But this conclufion is alfo wrong. For the anfwer here given, being directed to JOHN himfelf, plainly fhews, that He, and not his difciples, was chiefly concerned in the inquiry.

Accordingly, others again have imagined, that the whole is the Baptift's own tranfaction; who, being now, they fuppofe, depreffed in mind, and impatient of confinement, fent this meffage to our Saviour in a fullen mood, as thinking himfelf overlooked and neglected. For thus they interpret the words. "If thou art "the Christ," one of whofe characters it is, "to proclaim liberty to the captives, "and the opening of the prifon to them "that are bound; how is it, that I, who "prepared thy way before thee, am now "fuffered to lie thus ufelefs in prifon; and "not rather releafed, even by a miracle, "to be further affifting in the propaga- "tion of Religion?" But this interpretation alfo, is as far diftant from the truth of the cafe, as it is difcordant from the Baptift's conduct.

## SERMON III.

The conduct of the Baptist was always sedate; and all his proceedings were ever conformable to the state and condition of things. The message which he now sent to CHRIST, was founded on a peculiar circumstance: and, however it may sound at first hearing, was certainly meant, not to bring our SAVIOUR's title into doubt; but to set it in a clear and proper light. The ground of the Baptist's question lay in this.—He had received a revelation from Heaven, which assured him, that " upon " whom he should *see* the Spirit *descending,* " and *remaining* upon him, the same is he " who is the son of GOD, and the promised " MESSIAH."

Now, JOHN saw the Spirit *descending* upon our SAVIOUR; and accordingly testified of him. But whether the Spirit still *remained* with him, and ever *resided* upon him:—

This was a point, which the Baptift, being always abfent, could not determine. And yet, it was the very point, of which it concerned him, for the completion of his teftimony, to be well afcertained. And the meffage, in reality, was nothing more than a requeft to be fatisfied in this particular.

The power of working miracles the Baptift readily allowed to be a full and clear manifeftation of the Spirit.—But fuch a power he himfelf had never feen exercifed by our SAVIOUR. When, therefore, he had heard in the prifon of fome miraculous works being done by CHRIST; as he could not go himfelf to be certified of them, he fent *two* of his difciples, as *legal* witneffes of what might happen; and by them faid unto JESUS—" Art thou he " that fhould come, or do we look for another?"

another?" that is, in other words, and in the Baptift's own language, I faw the Spirit defcending upon thee—but, Art thou he upon whom the Spirit was continually to remain? And canft thou, by working miracles, make it vifible to the world, that he ftill remaineth on thee? That this is the true fenfe and meaning of the queftion, is evident from the account that immediately follows: For thus the Evangelift proceeds—" And in that fame hour—in
" the very hour that the queftion was put
" to him, JESUS cured many of their in-
" firmities and plagues, and of evil fpirits;
" and unto many that were blind he gave
" fight." Then faid he unto the meffengers, " Go your way, and tell JOHN what
" things ye have feen and heard—how that
" the blind fee, the lame walk, the lepers
" are cleanfed, the deaf hear, the dead
" are

"are raised, and to the poor the Gospel "is preached."

From these miracles which the messengers had seen, and which they afterwards faithfully related, the baptist could not but conclude, that the Spirit still *remained* upon CHRIST, and that consequently he was the true Messiah—the real Person that was to come—nor were they to look for another. For the miracles performed by our SAVIOUR, are both for their number and quality, so peculiar to the MESSIAH, that they cannot be attributed to any other person. JOHN, being thus convinced, that JESUS was the person foretold by the Prophets, he now began, it seems, to infuse into his disciples the same opinion—to recommend him to their acknowledgment as the redeemer of Israel—and to perswade them to adopt him as their proper and
rightful

rightful mafter. This exhortation had its due and full effect upon them. For we find, that, after the Baptift's death, his difciples came to JESUS; followed him; and continued their attendance upon him.

In this light the whole tranfaction appears natural, reafonable, and interefting—what the circumftances of things led JOHN to do—and what when done, ultimately contributed to a glorious purpofe—to the confirmation of our SAVIOUR's divine miffion, and to the furtherance and advancement of his Gofpel in the world.

But notwithftanding the weight and validity of this additional and final teftimony, which the Baptift gave in favour of CHRIST; yet was it neceffary to obviate fome prejudices, which the populace might entertain againft it. Accordingly we read, that,

E 4 when

when the messengers of JOHN were departed, JESUS began to speak unto the people concerning JOHN, and concerning, what might appear to them, the seeming variableness of his conduct. The whole discourse, in connexion with what went before, may be thus paraphrased. " You went unto JOHN some time ago; and he bare express witness that I was the true MESSIAH.—You have heard the message which he sent now—and what would you deduce from thence?" Seems he to be " a reed shaken by the wind—" a man wavering in his testimony, and unstable in his opinion? No. You will find him uniformly steady and constant unto the end. Or, think you that he flattered me like a courtier, in hopes of being advanced to superior eminence in my supposed temporal kingdom? That you cannot think: for the austerity of his life, so contrary

## SERMON III.

trary to the softness of a court, is an evident proof, that he had no view to, nor any regard for, the honours, profits and pleasures of the world—and as plain a proof, that my kingdom, for which he prepared you, is not likewise of this world. What then are you to conclude? that he is a Prophet? yea; and a greater Prophet than any that went before him. For they prophesied only of my coming; but he pointed me out as already come—for of me he said, " behold the Lamb of God." But nevertheless, tho' among them that are *born* of *women*, there hath not arisen a greater Prophet than John the Baptist; yet be assured, that he who is *born* of the *Spirit*, and duly instructed in the Gospel-Doctrine, is far greater than he—knows several important truths, of which John could have no conception; and is enabled

to

to reach thofe fublimer virtues, for which JOHN was not fully qualified.

How clearly does this declaration affert the fuperiority of the Chriftian Religion over both the Religion of Nature and the Jewifh difpenfation? And how forcibly fhould it engage both Jews and infidels to examine with candour the merits of this Religion; and to yield it that affent and reverence, which its explored excellence juftly claims? For fore will be their condemnation, if, when light is come into the world, men ftill love to continue in darknefs, and to fhut their eyes againft that light. And juft will it be too. For they would never act in fo perverfe a manner, " unlefs their deeds were evil."

With refpect to ourfelves, who acknowledge the excellency of this Religion, and
pro-

profess it in its genuine purity; our great care and concern should be, that the uprightness of our lives may bear proportion to the equity of its precrpts; and our piety may be anfwerable to the fublimity of its doctrines. Our great care should be, to "add to our faith virtue; and to adorn "the doctrine of GOD our SAVIOUR in all "things." Our great care should be, to "make our light fo fhine before men, that "they may fee our good works;" and admiring their luftre, may be induced to perform the fame. And the more effectually to attain this glorious end, let it be our greateft care daily to fupplicate our heavenly Father, that he would "graft in our hearts the love of his name, "increafe in us true Religion, nourifh us "with all goodnefs, and of his great mercy "keep us in the fame, through JESUS "CHRIST our Lord."—To whom, &c.

SER-

# SERMON IV.

# SERMON IV.

### PROVERBS i.—20.

**WISDOM CRIETH WITHOUT: SHE UTTERETH HER VOICE IN THE STREETS.**

WHEN we reflect with ourselves of what great importance Religion is to the happiness of mankind, and how highly it concerns all its professors to be zealous and diligent in the practice of it; anxious for our own welfare, we may wish perhaps, that it had pleased the Almighty

to

to imprefs upon our minds a more lively fenfe of its weighty obligations; and to fix us, by fome means, in a more fteady courfe of obedience to its dictates:—that it had pleafed him, for example, to appoint thefe material objects, which furround us, as kind remembrancers of our fpiritual concerns; and fo to order the occurrences of life, that, whilft we are pafsing through things temporal, we might conftantly be reminded of the things that are eternal. For, having then—fuch a crowd of monitors perpetually about us, pointing to us our duty, and urging us to perform it, at every turn;—we may be led to imagine, that we fhould be no longer fubject to our prefent irregularities; but, directing our courfe to a proper end, fhould proceed invariably in the ways of righteoufnefs; and daily advance in piety and virtue.

But

## SERMON IV.

But, alas! how deceitful are thefe imaginations! since the truth is, that the very expedient we propofe, how little foever we may profit by it, is actually employed by our gracious Creator, to the great purpofe of fpiritual improvement. As we are placed in this world to be trained up and difciplined for eternity, fo the world itfelf is a kind of fchool, where every thing that occurs leads to wife and pious reflections—reads to us a conftant leffon of morality—and exhorts us to provide for our future good. For doth not Wifdom cry without, and utter her voice in the fields, and in the ftreets? Doth not every object we meet, and every event that happens, labour, as it were, to arreft our attention, and adminifter counfel to our wandering hearts? Is it not the cry of all Nature to the fons of men—" How long, ye fimple ones, will " ye love fimplicity; and, ye fcorners, de-
" light

"light in scorning; and fools hate know-
"ledge? Listen in time to the voice of
"reproof; attend speedily to the checks
"which Providence has placed in your
"giddy course; and be persuaded thereby
"to suspend your pursuits, and turn your
"feet into the way of godliness."

Whatever irregularities we may be guilty of, and whatsoever disorders may be found in our conduct, nothing has been wanting on GOD's part to make us wiser and better men. That mercy, which is over all his works, and that paternal care which he exerts over the creatures of his hands, is in no instance more visible, than in the plentiful provision he has graciously made, both for the discovery of his sacred will, and for enforcing conformity to it. In all the several adjustments of his wisdom at the creation of the world, and in all the

the various difpenfations of his providence from that to the prefent time, He has fhewn throughout a manifeft regard to this important article. For he has made it, as it fhould feem, his peculiar bufinefs to addrefs his voice to the children of men; —to teach and direct them—to admonifh and exhort them—and all with this view, that they might live well and virtuoufly here, in order to be perfect and happy hereafter.

This He has done, and continues to do, by all imaginable methods. For man has not more capacities for receiving the revelations of God, than the means are, which God makes ufe of, to reveal himfelf to him. " He fpeaks to him fleeping, " and he fpeaks to him waking. He " fpeaks to him in company, and he " fpeaks to him in retirement. He fpeaks " to

" to his senses, and he speaks to his un-
" derstanding. He speaks to him within,
" and he speaks to him without: within,
" by the silent dictates of reason, and the
" secret whispers of conscience; without,
" by the visible frame and order of the
" universe—by the Heavens, which declare
" the glory of God, and by the Earth
" that abounds with his riches. He speaks
" to him also by the course of human af-
" fairs—by the histories of former times,
" and by the transactions of his own. He
" speaks to him by his judgments, and by
" his mercies—by the rewards that are
" conferred on good men, and by the
" punishments inflicted on the wick-
" ed. He speaks to him by the counsels
" and admonitions of friends, and by the
" reproaches and revilings of enemies. He
" speaks to him by every good book he
" reads, and by every sermon he hears.

" Fi-

## SERMON IV.

"Finally, he speaks to him, and O that
"he would attend!—he speaks to him in
"the most emphatical manner, by that
"express revelation he has made of his
"will in the holy Scriptures: by Moses,
"and by the Prophets, by Christ, and by
"his Apostles; by the Law, and by the
"Gospel."

By these, and many other ways, does God speak and address himself to mankind: and whatever he says to us by any of these ways, we should diligently weigh and ponder in our minds;—especially what is said and revealed by the ministry of the Gospel. For here Wisdom truly cries, and Understanding exerts her voice. Because, here the eternal wisdom of the Father, the divine Logos himself, the second person in the glorious Trinity, who is the great luminary of the intellectual

world

world, affuming our nature, and becoming, as it were, a fenfible light, condefcends to inftruct us after the manner of men; —to teach us our duty in the moft familiar terms—to lead us to the performance of it by his own example—and to encourage us to follow him by the moft alluring rewards. And confidering the qualifications of this great inftructor—his acquaintance with the human heart, and the propriety of his applications—what fruit might we not expect from the feed fown by fo fkilful an hand? But, as at the firft, the cares of life—thofe thorns nd briers—choaked the word in fome, and its vain pleafures—thofe fowls of the air—devoured it up in others; even fo it is now. The vanities and follies of every kind, which engaged thofe who lived before us, ftill prevail, through our own negligence, in equal degree over ourfelves—

work

work upon our affections—and bring us into captivity to the law of sin. We, as well as they, would fain indeed excuse our faults, and palliate our crimes under the cover of infirmities. For how often do we hear it alleged, that the world is so fraught with temptations on every side, and our appetites are so eager to embrace them, that it is next to impossible to maintain our ground, and keep from falling, in such circumstances? But, what is this in effect, but to charge God foolishly; and defend our own wickedness at the expence of divine goodness, and certainly at the expence of truth? For, if the world is adapted to work upon our passions, is it not equally adapted to work upon our reason too? If it supplies us with incentives to vice, does it not afford us as strong motives and encouragements to virtue?

tue? Indeed, if properly confidered, it moves and perfuades us to nothing elfe.

For look into its various parts, and confider their feveral tendencies, do they not all refer us ultimately to GOD, and remind us daily of our duty to Him? Do they not all fuggeft to us the moft noble fubjects for prayer and meditation, and tend to make our whole lives a continued feries of devotion? No fooner does the fun rife to our view, and create the day for us, but it awakens the thoughts of every ferious foul, and brings to his remembrance that fun of righteoufnefs, who chafed away the darknefs of error, and enlightened the world with the knowledge of falvation. And, whilft we enjoy the *light* of the day, are we not put in mind of the *work* of the day, the important work of him that fent us, which muft be done before it is night?
—Does

—Does not every clock that we hear ftrike —founding the knell of departed hours— inform us of the neceffity of doing it fpeedily, and fetting about it without delay?— How forcibly does the Spring, that feafon of the year, in which we prepare and cultivate the ground for the future crop we expect from it; excite us to improve the feafon of youth, that feed-time of life in which we receive thofe actuating principles, that afterwards govern our maturer conduct? For it is as true in the moral, as in the natural fenfe, that whatfoever a man foweth, that fhall he alfo reap.—Can the aged and hoary head—lift up his eyes, and look on the fields, all white and ready for harveft; and not queftion himfelf, and with anxious concern, whether he ftands in the field of life, among the tares or among the wheat? knowing that death will fhortly come, and cut him down,

either

either to be deposited with the one in the granary, or condemned with the others to the fire.—If we turn about to the transactions of the world, the like instructions still crowd upon us. Every traveller we meet on the road, reminds us that we ourselves are travelling through life, having here no fixed abode; and that therefore we should set our faces right, and make the best of our journey to our destined home. When we observe our fellow-creatures rising up early, and labouring so hard for the meat that perisheth; are we not admonished to exert our endeavours, and secure that meat which endureth to everlasting life?—When we see men eager in pursuit of wealth, heaping up fruitless and fading treasures, are we not led to consider the necessity of acquiring the true riches, and of laying up in store for ourselves a good foundation against the time

to

to come ?—And with refpect to that time, are we not moved to reflect on what will be our lot, by the impreffions that are made on our fouls at prefent? Have we not fome fpecimen daily given us of the happinefs and mifery that await us hereafter, in the enjoyments and fufferings we experience here ? And do not thofe fenfations—the pleafure we love, and the pain we hate—loudly warn us to take care of ourfelves, and to adjuft our conduct after fuch a manner, that we may at laft be happy, and not miferable in that future ftate, which is either all happinefs, or all mifery for ever ?

Thus it is that the Almighty calls up all nature to our affiftance, to put us in mind of what we fhould do, and keep us fteady to the performance of it. The vain and the thoughtlefs indeed, who look only on

the

the *vail* of nature, and admire it for nothing but its gay colouring, will gather from thence but little inftruction, though it exhibits to them a lively picture of the fading glories of human life. Blinded with the glare of outward fhow, and intent on the Follies that are current in the world, they will ftill purfue and carefs their pleafures, though the rofes and flowers with which they deck and adorn themfelves, would fain inftruct them by their quick decay, " fo to number their days, that they may apply their hearts unto wifdom." But others, it is to be hoped, of a more ferious turn, look into the things beneath the vail—confider their ufe in a fpiritual light—and find by experience how well they are adapted both for correction, and inftruction in Righteoufnefs—How well they are adapted—to keep alive a fenfe of duty—to quicken us in the difcharge of it—

it—and make us ready unto every good work—How well they are adapted—to *difengage* our affections from the world—to lead and raise them up to God—and prepare us for the life of Heaven. And let those who despise this art of life, and make light of these silent calls of Nature, remember that the time is coming on, when, devoid of the improvements they *might* have made, they shall heartily wish, they had used the world to better purpose.—For when the delirium of the senses, and the hurry of the passions, are once allayed, and sickness or distress will soon allay them, things will appear in a different light: the world and its vanities will sink upon our hands,—and we shall see the importance of all these applications that God makes, and how greatly it behoves us to comply with them. For it is not his *own suit* that he thus earnestly solicits with us,

neither

neither is it for his *own advantage* that he makes thefe continual appeals to us. But it is *our intereſt*, and *our concern* that he efpoufes; and as it is *to* us he fpeaks, fo it is *for* us, and for our fupreme good. That which he defires is—that we would be happy; and that we would take fuch a courfe as will make us fo. That we would live and act wifely and like ourfelves, that is, like rational creatures. That we would fit and difpofe ourfelves for the happinefs he has provided for us—bring ourfelves within the compafs of his love and mercy— and fo demean ourfelves for this fhort time, that he may reward us with a bleffed eternity.

See then, my brethren, that ye refufe not him that fpeaketh fuch things. For if you do, the confequence ſtands clofe to the words of my text, and is delivered in alarming

ming language. "Becaufe I have called and ye refufed, I have ftretched out my hand and no man regarded; but ye have fet at nought my counfel, and would none of my reproof: I alfo will laugh at your calamity; I will mock when your fear cometh:— when your fear cometh as defolation, and your deftruction cometh as a whirlwind:— when diftrefs and anguifh cometh upon you." Reflect, I befeech you, on the diftreffed hour of your diffolution—how ready you will be then to call upon GOD, and how *defirous* that he fhould anfwer you? Reflect alfo on the great and terrible Day of Judgment, when you *muft* and *fhall* hear him in his fentence upon you. And, as you wifh, that GOD may hear *you* readily at the hour of your death, and you may hear *him* with comfort in the day of his Judgment; fo take care to hearken now to his

his voice, whilft he affectionately befpeaks you by fuch a variety of inftruction.

" Whofo is wife will ponder thefe things; " and they fhall underftand the loving-" kindnefs of the LORD."—His kindnefs in providing fo amply for our improvement here; his kindnefs in rewarding us for making that improvement with eternal happinefs hereafter. Amen.

SERMON

# SERMON V.

# SERMON V.

EPHESIANS iv.—12.

—FOR THE EDIFYING OF THE BODY OF CHRIST.

THE Religion which Christ introduced into the world, though at first confined to his immediate followers, was plainly intended for the general benefit of mankind. In order therefore that mankind might partake of the benefit intended by it, our Saviour commanded his disciples to " go forth into all the world, " and *preach* the Gospel to every creature." Endowed and qualified for the work, " they " went forth accordingly, and preached " every where ; the Lord working with " them, and confirming the word with " signs following."

By these means the Gospel was speedily conveyed and propagated over diverse countries. But into whatever country it might be thus introduced, if it had been left with the inhabitants without any *support* ;—without any *settled* method for *preserving* and *perpetuating* the knowledge of it; how very soon would it have begun to decline ?—Nay, how soon indeed would it have totally sunk—neglected, and forgotten ? For, what reason is there to imagine, that the doctrine of our Saviour, how-

however recommended at its firft promulgation, would have fared better, or been more effectually retained and practifed, than the doctrine of the *ancient philofophers*; if, like that, it had been only a fyftem of fpeculative principles and moral precepts, fimply propofed to every man's own *private* ftudy and *perfonal* application? Tranfmitted to writing, the Gofpel, we grant, might have been always known to a few curious and inquifitive perfons: but the reft of the world—the great body of mankind, would ftill have remained almoft as entirely ignorant of it, as if no fuch doctrine had ever been revealed. For the generality of the people in every place are fo employed in the toilfome and laborious works of life, that they have not leifure for acquiring the knowledge of ancient writings in the way of refearch and ftudy: if ever they attain to any knowledge of them, they muft chiefly attain it by the help and affiftance of *living inftructors*, and by fuch methods and forms as are properly adapted to convey into their minds the fentiments and notions which thofe writings contain.

Hence then we fee the expedience and neceffity of *external rites* and *eftablifhed appointments*, as the moft effectual means of propagating and preferving the knowledge of Religion, and rendering it fubfervient to thofe important purpofes, which it is gracioufly intended to promote. And accordingly we find, that *formal acts* and *ritual obfervances*, of one kind or other, made a part of every Religion that has ever yet obtained a footing in the world. The *Jewifh* Religion abounded with them; from whence our Saviour felected thofe that were of general ufe, and adopted them into his own inftitution. For it pleafed him,

him, we may obferve, to form believers into one body; and to unite them in one vifible community; where they profeffed his Religion in a *common form* of *worſhip*, and had the principles of it impreffed on their minds by a regular method of inftruction. This is evident from the account we have of the firft Chriftian converts; who, when they were baptized, are faid to have " continued firm and fteadfaft " in the Apoftles doctrine and fellowſhip, " and in breaking of bread, and in prayers." They all made, you fee, one *church*, or *religious ſociety*; they all lived together in *one viſible* external *communion*, where they attended the difcourfes and inftructions of the Apoftles—partook of the facrament of the Lord's Supper—and offered up to God their united prayers and thankfgivings.

Such was the constitution of this primitive Church: and it appears from the words preceding the text, that all the rest were afterwards formed on the same model: having every one of them a standing ministry of instruction and discipline, together with a common stated form of *public* worship. For, as sure as our Lord appointed some APOSTLES and EVANGELISTS, to spread abroad the knowledge of his Gospel, and plant Churches in different parts; so sure is it, that, wherever they *were* planted and established, he appointed others PASTORS and TEACHERS;—whose office it was to preside in the several assemblies of Christians—to direct the people in the outward exercise of their devotion—to instruct them in the nature of the Religion they professed—to explain to them the duties it required at their hands—and to

ex-

excite them to the practice and observance of them.

Under the influence of this œconomy, and by means of these institutions, Christianity advanced and flourished:—the knowledge of it was diffused through all ranks and degrees of men; and brought forth among them the genuine fruits of good living. Now it is happily come down to *us*, the like effects may be reasonably expected. For whatever those establishments were which contributed so effectually to the growth and advancement of the Christian Religion in former times; yet this to our comfort is certain—that no institution, or mode of worship established in any place, was better calculated to edify the Church, and improve its members in grace and knowledge, than are the forms and service of our own communion.

In proof of this I am naturally led to display its excellencies, as an edifying service. But all its excellencies in this respect are not to be comprised in the compass of a short discourse; and therefore a few of the most obvious will, I trust, be sufficient to shew, in what high estimation we ought to hold it, and with what zealous attachment we should preserve the use of it.

And here let it be considered as its first excellency, that our Book of Common Prayer is composed in our *common language*— in a plain and easy style, adapted to the comprehension of the meanest capacities, and yet fully answerable to the sentiments of the highest.

Being thus intelligible to all orders and degrees of men, and fitted to convey instruction; the next valuable property of

it

## SERMON V.

it is—that it actually conveys the beſt and moſt uſeful inſtructions to us. It acquaints us with the Nature and Perfections of GOD; ſome of whoſe Attributes are conſtantly ſet forth in the *Preface* of all our Prayers. It ſhews us the Dignity and Power of our Saviour; in whoſe *Name* we put up our Petitions, and on whoſe *Merits* we rely for the acceptance of them. It informs us of the Offices of the HOLY SPIRIT, whoſe Grace we invoke, and whoſe Aid we implore, to enable us to maintain our Chriſtian warfare.

And as we are thus inſtructed with regard to the *Object* of our Faith and Worſhip; and taught to acknowledge the *whole Trinity*; ſo is this Faith and Acknowledgment daily revived and confirmed in us by the repeated uſe of that ancient form, which aſcribes *glory* to each perſon.—

fon—A form never more neceffary to be retained; than in this free-*thinking*, and this free-*speaking* age, when the *Divinity* of *Chriſt* and of the *Holy Ghoſt* is become the fubject, not *only* of *contradiction*, but, fhameful infolence! even of *mirth* and *ridicule*.

Next to the Knowledge of GOD, the moft important is the knowledge of *ourſelves*; which is frequently inculcated in our public liturgy. For we are thereby reminded of the corruption of our nature, and our own inability to cleanfe and purify it: we are taught to bewail our vilenefs and depravity, and inſtructed in the only method that is capable of advancing us to a purer ſtate. This fenſe of our conſtant dependance on the Almighty for all things neceffary both to life and godlinefs, naturally leads us to approach him with reverence—to confefs our fins to him with the deepeſt

deepest sorrow and humiliation—to supplicate for future mercies with a pious deference to his will—and to acknowledge with sincere gratitude the blessings we have received. And in all these acts how admirably are we assisted by the prayers of our church! which at the same time that they are adapted to make us devout, have a strong tendency to keep us obedient.

To direct our obedience in the course of life, we have certain portions of scripture daily read to us; which not only bring us instruction in some particular branch of righteousness, but also encourage us, by various motives, to the faithful performance of it. Nay, so concerned is our Church for the interest of virtue, and the advancement of holiness, that its devotions have all a *practical* aspect; and, whilst they lead us to *adore* and *praise* God for his goodness,

ness, shew us our obligations to fulfil his commands. The very petitions we make for a supply of the common necessaries of life, perpetually remind us, by the *turn* of their expressions, of the common duties of it: so that it is impossible for us attentively to join in the public worship, without being confirmed in the justest notions both of God and ourselves;—without being excited to a true repentance of our past sins, and to a regular conduct in our future proceedings.

All these things, and many more to the same effect, our liturgy strongly inculcates. And since it is allowed that it does inculcate them, is it not surprising that men should be so perverse as to charge it with deficiences in point of edification? For in what does the work of edification consist? Does it not evidently consist in confirming our faith,

faith, and improving our morals—in bringing us to the knowledge of the doctrines of religion, and promoting our growth in chriftian graces? But, if our *Faith* is to be confirmed, by what means can it be better eftablifhed, than by rehearfing continually the *articles* of it? If our *morals* are to be improved, what method can be devifed more conducive to that purpofe, than to bring them to the *teft* of God's *Commandments?* And what greater inducements can we have to encourage us to go on in welldoing, than the motives of the gofpel, and the example of Christ which are fet before us in the daily leffons? If our difpofitions are to be changed, and rendered more pious, what can be more fuitably adapted to the promotion of that end, than thofe pure and refined devotions of our church, which breathe the nobleft and moft animating fervours, at the fame time that they are

tem-

tempered with all the coolnefs of fobriety and judgment? Laftly if we would fhew our gratitude, difplay our love, and return our thanks to GOD for his mercies, what better help can we poffibly want to affift us in thefe exalted acts of adoration, than that which we receive from the pfalms of DAVID, which are fully expreffive of our devouteft thoughts and applicable to all our conditions?

We may appeal then to the unprejudiced reafon of mankind—whether the public offices of our Church have not a plain and powerful tendency to ftrengthen and improve good principles; and to form a temper of fincere piety and folid virtue in all who carefully attend to them; and whether it be indeed poffible, for any one long to attend to them with judgment and affection, without finding himfelf much improved

proved in this temper by them? Nay, we may further appeal to the *experience* of the world, whether many perfons of low capacities and mean fituations have not been raifed by thefe fervices to an eminent degree of wifdom and virtue? And whether even men of the moſt refined underſtandings, and the moſt noble difpofitions, do not receive an additional relifh of what is good, and frefh vigour for the purfuit of it, from their due attendance on thefe folemnities?

If edification therefore be, " to go on to-
" wards perfection, and to grow in grace,
" and the knowledge of our SAVIOUR, JE-
" SUS CHRIST ;"—if it be, to make plain the doctrines of Religion to the underſtandings of men, and to urge its precepts home on their hearts ;—if it be, to awaken them to a fenfe of their duty, and to keep them

H          ſtead-

steadfast to the practice of it;—if *these* be "the things, which are good" and proper "to the use of edifying,"—then I am sure better edification cannot be found in *any* church now upon earth, than in our *own*.

Let *us* then, who are members of this excellent church, where GOD is worshipped in so rational and becoming a manner; and where there is so ample a provision made for our own improvement in virtue and piety; let *us*, I say, rejoice in our lot, and learn to value our own happiness. Let us be careful to make a right use of the opportunities we enjoy; and endeavour to profit by a constant, serious and devout attendance on the public worship.

For in vain is this provision made for us; in vain do we boast of the excellency of our liturgy, if we neglect to join in the services of of it. And yet, to our great reproach as well as detriment, the " forsaking the assembling " of ourselves together" for the purposes of public worship, is become now, not only " the manner of some," but even a *prevailing* fashion. And what has been the consequence of this presumptuous neglect, but a visible, and to serious men an alarming decay of every thing that is good and praise-worthy? For, ever since we have learned to profane the sabbath, and withdraw ourselves from the services of the church, how unsettled have we been in our religious principles! and how irregular in our moral practices! But indeed what wonder? since by neglecting the public worship of the church, we neglect the principal means of knowledge, and the most effectual institution that can well be contrived for our improvement in virtue and goodness.

But then if we mean to improve by it, we muſt be ſure to attend with an inward ſerioufneſs and devotion of mind. This is a qualification abſolutely neceſſary to render the performance of theſe religious duties either acceptable to GOD, or beneficial to ourſelves. For notwithſtanding their natural fitneſs to excite in us pious thoughts, and to urge us on to virtuous actions; yet the efficacy of them entirely depends on the good diſpoſitions we bring with us to the celebration of them. And it is owing to the want of theſe diſpoſitions, and not to any defect in the compoſition itſelf, that the ſervice of the church has ſo little influence on numbers of thoſe, who attend it. A want that we ſhould by all means labour to remove;—as well for the ſake of our own advantage, as for the honour of that eſtabliſhment, which we would be thought to admire. If we en-

gage

gage in the duties of public worship, as a thing of courſe, and without a due preparation of mind, the moſt ſolemn acts of our devotion will prove but dead forms—a mere "bodily exerciſe," that will have no virtue in it at all either to recommend us to the acceptance of GOD, or to produce any good effect on ourſelves. Hence the ſtill-remaining corruption of our lives will be made an argument—has been urged indeed as the principal proof—of the unprofitableneſs of the form we uſe : becauſe many of us appear to be very little *edifyed* by it, therefore it has been concluded, that our ſervice is really unedifying. But if the paſt courſe of your lives has unhappily contributed to ſtrengthen this prejudice againſt our liturgy, pray be ſo kind to yourſelves and your religion as to endeavour to confute it by your future conduct. Be zealouſly conſtant in your attendance at church;

church; and when you are there, join in the prayers of it with becoming reverence; and liften to the inftructions you hear delivered with proper attention. When you come out into the world, let the light and inftruction you have received fhine forth in your converfation. Then, perhaps, thofe who diffent from us, feeing our good works, may be induced thereby to follow us to *this* place to glorify our great and common Father. Then may we hope, that *all* will come to that *unity* of faith and worfhip,—and to that ftrength, maturity and perfection of goodnefs, which CHRIST, by calling us into the fellowfhip of his Gofpel, defigned to raife us.

# SERMON VI.

# SERMON VI.

### LUKE iii. 4.

PREPARE YE THE WAY OF THE LORD, MAKE HIS PATHS STRAIGHT.

WHEN the time arrived in which the Jews expected the appearance of their Messiah; his forerunner, JOHN the Baptist, earnestly exhorted them, as his office led him, so to fit and prepare themselves, that they might give him a proper and worthy reception:—that they might be ready to embrace

embrace the terms and conditions, on which they were to become the fubjects;—and, if they proved faithful, would inherit the privileges of that kingdom, which he was then come to erect in the world. Though CHRIST came to his own, with glad and glorious tidings; to which *they* fhould have joyfully attended, above all *other* people; yet even *his own*, the Baptift well knew would never receive him—would never fubmit to his government and laws—unlefs their prejudices, their errours and vices were firft corrected and removed;—and their minds previoufly difpofed for the admiffion of truth and virtue.

He calls therefore upon them in the words of the prophet, and gives them to underftand—that " every valley fhould be " filled, and every mountain and hill " fhould be brought low;—that the crook-
" ed

## SERMON VI.

" ed should be made straight, and the
" rough places smooth ;—if they wished
" to see the salvation of GOD."—In plainer
terms,—that the *low* conception they entertained of the end and design of the
MESSIAH's appearance, as operating only
to their temporal deliverance, should be
*raised* to something more truly worthy of
the character he sustained ;—and that the
*exalted* expectation they cherished, of seeing him shine in the regal pomp of a
mighty conqueror, should be *brought down*
to the standard of reason, and the nature
of that Spiritual Kingdom, which the
Prophets foretold he was finally to establish ;—that they should *rectify* those *crooked*
and *perverse* dispositions, which, in consequence of these mistaken views, they had
unhappily contracted ;—and *smooth* those
*rugged* and refractory tempers, which they
were too apt to indulge ;—before they
could

could be fit and equitable judges, either of the proofs which Christ brought of his divine miffion; or of the truth of the doctrine, which he delivered to the world.

It is not fufficient towards making men believers—it is not fufficient towards making them *chriftians*, that they have the Gofpel tendered, and the terms of Salvation propofed to them, even by Christ himfelf. No Arguments will have any effect upon them, unlefs their minds be fo prepared; fo freed from all vicious prejudices; unlefs they be moulded into fuch a frame and temperament, as to be fufceptible of good impreffions; and ready to yield to fuch proofs and motives as ought to operate their conviction.

When Christ appeared among the Jews, diftinguifhed by all the concurring marks of of the true Messiah;—when he came to them at the expected time; answered the types; fulfilled the prophecies; performed miracles; and received immediate testimonies from Heaven; yet, their prejudices had so obstructed, so blinded their eyes, that they could see no signs of *his* being the person " that should have come;"—and therefore they despised and rejected him.— And though He spake such comfortable things, as never man spake before, to the admiration and astonishment of the less prejudiced vulgar; yet the meanness of his birth, and the place of his abode were looked upon by the malicious chiefs,—by the scribes and pharisees,—as unanswerable objections to his miracles and doctrine.

The case is the same in every age—whilst any carnal impediment; whilst any vicious passion; whilst any wrong habit, keeps pos-

possession of the human mind, it will be sure to block up all its avenues;—and to prevent every thing that is serious, spiritual and religious from entering in. Let the doctrine be ever so good; let it be applied with ever so much skill, dexterity and diligence; it will nevertheless depend at last on the temper and disposition of those who hear it, whether it shall be attended with effect.

What doctrines can be more reasonable; what doctrines can be more worthy of GOD, and more beneficial to men, than those doctrines of humility, meekness, resignation, contentedness, purity, patience and piety, which our SAVOUR preached to the *Jews?* yet, notwithstanding their propriety, their excellence and sublimity; the Jews, who were egregiously proud and vain; notoriously covetous and wordly-minded;

minded; who were full of deceit, hypocrisy and malice; disrelished and despised his sayings.

All the awakening truths they heard; all the astonishing miracles they saw; were so far from working their conviction, that, by a perverse and wilful misapplication, they served but to increase their obstinacy; and to harden them in those sins and errours, which finally terminated in their misery and ruin.

These things happened to the Jews for ensamples; and they are written for our admonition;—to the intent, that *we* may be more careful to prepare ourselves to meet our LORD, than *they* were formerly.

CHRIST comes now *virtually* to *us*; as in time past he *personally* came to *them*: and there-

therefore it behoves us, to be ready to give him a fit reception. He comes to *us* now in his word and ordinances; and it concerns us, diligently to attend to his word, and faithfully to obferve his ordinances.

We know to whom the word was preached; and yet, did not profit them: and we know the reafons of its proving fruitlefs. With this knowledge, let us firmly bear in mind, that the fame caufes will always produce the fame effects:—that the fame prejudices, lufts and paffions, that prompted the *Jews* to oppofe our Saviour, and to reject his Gofpel; will, wherever they take place, lead other men to follow their example:—to think lightly of the Chriftian Religion, to live in a contemptuous neglect of its ordinances, and in open violation of its laws and precepts.

This

This is an alarming confideration—and ought to put every one of us on his guard, againſt all ſinful tempers and perverſe habits, that bear any affinity to thoſe of the Jews; which were the great obſtacles at firſt to their receiving the MESSIAH; and the great impediments afterwards to their believing his doctrines.

If the mean opinion, which the Jews entertained of CHRIST, on account of his low appearance, led them to defpife him, as a perſon unfit to be their SAVIOUR; let us take warning from hence, that we never ſuffer the high conceptions we have of our own reaſon, to difparage the plainneſs and ſimplicity of the Gofpel; or to think it an unlikely fcheme of falvation.

If a bafe and fordid love of the world, tempted the Phariſees to turn a deaf ear to our

Sa-

Saviour's fublime and heavenly doctrines; let us take heed, and beware of covetoufnefs;—and indeed of every immoderate attachment to the things of earth; left we be carried by intereft to deny the faith; or be tempted by profit to tranfgrefs the commands of God in practice. For, we find from early times, that when " the " cares of this world, the deceitfulnefs of " riches, and the luft of other things, " enter in," and take poffeffion of the heart; they are fure to choke every good principle, and to render fruitlefs every good inftruction. Thofe who are eager in laying up for themfelves treafures on earth, even the promife of an " inheritance incorruptible in the heavens" cannot affect. This world is the whole of their care; and godlinefs is to them nothing, unlefs it can be made an inftrument of gain. But further—

If

If pride and self-conceit, if a vain affectation of superior knowledge, prevented the Scribes from coming to Christ, and listening to his plain and easy discourses; let us then be admonished, " not to think " more highly of ourselves than we ought " to think, but to think soberly "—" cast- " ing down all vain imaginations and pre- " sumptuous reasonings, that would op- " pose the revelation of God; and bring- " ing into captivity every swelling thought " to the obedience of the Gospel of " Christ;" and forming our practice by the example of that master, who was so peculiarly " meek and lowly" both in mind and manners. Finally,

If hypocrisy and malice had so blinded the Jews, that they could not discern the light of the Gospel, even when it shone around them: If their hypocrisy had obscured and well-nigh extinguished all sense of religion and morality among them; and if their malice was continually plotting against *Him*, who compassionately laboured to work their reformation; with how jealous an eye should *we* watch over ourselves, that these vices may not infect us! For they are vices, you see, that will directly lead us to " turn the grace of GOD into wicked-" ness;" and to reject the good purpose of his benevolence, to our eternal and unspeakable detriment.

We know the certainty, we know the importance, of the word of GOD; let this therefore engage us to pay it a becoming regard; " and, laying aside all malice, and " all guile, and hypocrisy; as new-born " babes"—as persons of sincere and open hearts—let us " desire" that spiritual nourishment rifhment, that " fincere milk of the word, " which will make us grow to perfection."

The Gofpel was gracioufly defigned, for our improvement in virtue and goodnefs; and is admirably adapted to promote that end. And, therefore, when faithfully propofed, if it ever fails of its defired fuccefs, it is not owing to any defect or infufficiency in itfelf; but to the faults and indifpofition of thofe, to whom it is fo addreffed;—to fome wrong turn of thought, or fome perverfenefs of mind, which either obftructs or corrupts it.

Since then, it is of fuch mighty and important confequence, that we receive the word of GOD into found and perfect hearts; let us always be careful to preferve *ours* in fuch a frame and pofture—free to admit, and willing to cherifh good inftruction;

ready and difpofed to put that inftruction in practice.

If we have already received the feed—the feed of eternal life—into good ground; let us diligently cultivate it, that it may bring forth the fruits of good living. Let us continually attend to that good ground; and fee that it dos not degenerate.—Let us fuffer neither briers, thorns, nor baneful weeds, to grow up in it; but let us continually improve it into that condition, which is likely to promote its increafe and harveft. To fpeak without a metaphor. Let us always be prepared to receive found doctrine; and ready to adopt thofe facred rules, which our Lord has given us for the government of our lives and actions: And let us guard with all poffible caution againft thofe dangerous and deceitful errors which may lead us, firft, into a ftate of lukewarmness—into a state of indifference about religion; and then by degrees into a shameful neglect;—perhaps, at last, into a fatal contempt of God's word and commandment. The loose principles of the world, believe me, are no fit guides for those, who are on their passage to eternity. It is the Gospel that should direct us; because it is the Gospel only that can lead us to happiness. To the Gospel therefore let us constantly attend: studiously avoiding, or industriously correcting every false, though fashionable opinion, that has any tendency to obscure its truth; or to diminish its influence upon our lives.

Let us rule our hears with the utmost diligence; for in the heart is seated all religion; and out of it proceed the issues of life. As we have received Christ by faith; and perfectly know " the right ways of the

" Lord;

"Lord;" let us imitate his example;— and labour to make our own ways,— "*ſtraight*," and conformable with his. Let us ſtrive to rectify all the obliquities; and to correct all the wrong difpoſitions of our nature: that, being freed from theſe ſinful propenſities, we may become more ready, more willing, and more faithful ſervants of God:—and, having had our fruit unto holineſs here, may attain to everlaſting happineſs hereafter; through Jesus Christ our Lord.

# SERMON VII.

# SERMON VII.

### JOHN ix. 4.

I MUST WORK THE WORKS OF HIM THAT SENT ME, WHILE IT IS DAY: THE NIGHT COMETH, WHEN NO MAN CAN WORK.

THESE are the words of our blessed Saviour, who was sent into the world upon an office or employment peculiar to himself. The office he had undertaken was that of *redeeming* the world. In pursuance of this office the work he had to do, was

was to difplay the glory of God in the recovery and improvement of mankind. His work was, to reftore men to a capacity of attaining falvation;—to inftruct them in their duty by his doctrine;—and to guide them into the practice of it by his example. This commandment he received from his Father; and this he fulfilled, in the day of his miniftration, with fuch diligence and fidelity, that, when the night of his paffion approached, he could appeal with confidence to him that fent him in thefe folemn words—" I have glorified thee on " earth : I have finifhed the work thou " gaveft me to do."

Happy, could his difciples clofe their lives with the fame expreffions! For what our Saviour, in my text, declares of himfelf, is, in a qualified fenfe, truly applicable to all his followers. Notwithftanding the

the great things CHRIST has done for us, we have still—a work to do. CHRIST has, appointed our work, and bound it upon us: and we are sent into the world on purpose to do it. He has opened to us the way of salvation. It concerns us to work it out in the way he has shewn. It concerns us to work it out speedily, "while it is day; for the night cometh, "when no man can work."

But, to convince you the more fully of this truth, and to urge you to a suitable conduct, I shall endeavour in the

First place to shew, that GOD sent us, every one, into this world to do some work.

Secondly, that the work we have to do, is the work of GOD that sent us.

And

And to engage your diligence in the performance of this work, I shall shew in the

Third place, that it must be accomplished within the short term of this present life;—
" while it is day: for the night of death
" cometh, when we can no longer work."

I am first then to prove to you, that God sent us, every one, into this world to do some work.

Now, with this view, let me entreat you to consider, what kind of beings we are; and with what faculties endowed. We are active and reasonable creatures: capable of knowing the hand that formed us; and capable of doing our Maker service. Having then such faculties and powers, can we think them given us for no end? Are we *able* to do much, and yet

yet *obliged* to do nothing? Does not ability in its very nature imply duty? And muft we not conclude of courfe, that we are *bound* to act, when God has endowed us with capacities for action?

This neceffarily follows from the *nature* of our endowments, and is further confirmed to us by the exigencies of our condition.

We are placed in a world where our happinefs and welfare are made to depend on our own agency. Every period of our lives is fubject to continual wants. Thefe wants daily and hourly call upon us to exert ourfelves for the fupply of them. But this fupply cannot be procured without induftry; for fuch is the conftitution of things, that if any perfon will not work, neither fhall he eat.

Be-

Besides, as one stage of life is introductory to another, so are there services appropriated to each stage, necessary to be performed in order to prepare and qualify us for the succeeding. Youth must be industrious in its preparations for the offices of maturer age. Manhood must be industrious, not only in the discharge of its peculiar calling, but also in collecting and storing observations for the guidance of its future conduct. Nor has even old age a dispensation for idleness: It is bound to work: it must still act in example and in counsel:—It must shew the world what ought to be done; and employ its wisdom for the use of the ignorant and inexperienced. In this view life appears to have been intended by its Author, as a continued scene of activity; proceeding on from work to work through the whole extent and continuance of it. Every season, every situ-

## SERMON VII.

situation, and every state has its engagements;—calls upon us to exert ourselves, and to fill up the circle of our duty.

Some work then we, all of us, have to do; some business to complete. But the difficulty is not so much to convince our judgments that we are to act at all, as to engage our affections that we may act aright. Something we are always ready to do from the mere activity of our nature; but that something may prove at last neither agreeable to our duty, nor answerable to our pains. As all actions are not in themselves equally worthy, nor in their consequences equally beneficial; we should seriously reflect, before we engage in any work, what is becoming of, and what may be useful to us. For, otherwise, we shall labour on with a blind impetuosity,

and

and ruin ourselves by a perverseness of industry.

But if we give ourselves time to consider, we shall find—what I am now to prove in the

Second place, that the works which are worthy of us here, and will redound to our benefit hereafter, are those of God that sent us. They are called his works, not only, because he has enjoined them, but because himself also performs them. Would we then know what we must do, in order to work the works of God? Why, the point is clear—we must do as God does. For as he has designed us to be partakers of his glory, so he has appointed us to be fellow-workers with him. That we may then be properly directed in our labours, let us look up to God, and act as we have him for an example.  Now

Now, it is extremely visible in the scheme of providence, that God constantly adjusts his operations in a regular, though diversified manner, to the general good and preservation of the world. And since we are ordained to act as servants under him in the execution of his gracious plan, it should ever be our care to perform with diligence those various parts of it which he hath committed to our charge. These parts are assigned us with our stations. For our stations are the allotments of God; and if we mean to answer his intention of placing us in them, we must labour to promote the welfare of society; for without the benefits arising from our various occupations, the city cannot be inhabited, nor the state of the world preserved: and therefore every neglect in the business of our stations, is not only hurtful to ourselves, but also an injury

injury to the public, and a violation of the laws of God.

We are apt to confider our fecular employments in too contracted a light. We generally look upon them, as nothing more than the natural means of acquiring fubfiftence; whereas in truth they are fo many portions of the divine adminiftration; and reprefented in fcripture as fo many inftances of piety; the performance of which will entitle us to a reward, and the omiffion expofe us to punifhment.

Since then we are placed in the body civil, as the Apoftle obferves of the body fpiritual, for the mutual benefit of each other, and the perfection of the whole; it is every man's duty according to his circumftances to attend continually to that very thing. And " having gifts, differing according

ding to the grace given unto us; whether prophecy, let us prophefy according to the proportion of faith; or miniftry, let us wait on our miniftering; or, he that teacheth, on teaching; or he that exhorteth on exhortation: he that giveth, let him do it with fimplicity; he that ruleth, with diligence; he that fheweth mercy, with cheerfulnefs." In fhort: " Whatever our hand findeth to do," whatever bufinefs our proper ftation points out, we muft not be flothful in it, but muft do it with all our might, from a principle of confcience and fidelity. " This is wellpleafing to GOD; and at the fame time, good and profitable unto men."

But whilft we are employed in thefe works—the works of our feveral profeffions; let us bear in mind, that we have ftill a work, common to us all, of much higher concernment: the taking care of our souls, and preparing for eternity. This is peculiarly the work of God in which he hath interested himself throughout all ages. This is indeed the work, which we were sent into the world to do; and which if we leave undone, good had it been for us that we had not been sent into it. And yet a work it is, not to be accomplished by a few slight endeavours; not to be accomplished but by great labour and constant diligence; not to be accomplished but by the faithful use of the means prescribed, by resolution and perseverance. How many irregular inclinations have we, that are hard to be subdued? How many vicious habits that are harder to be rooted out? How many good dispositions have we that want to be cherished? How many virtues are there of difficult acquisition

sition to be ingrafted in our souls? Yet all these things, painful as they are, must be done. "The old man must be put off with all his corrupt and deceitful lusts; and the new man must be put on, adorned with righteousness and true holiness." We must, notwithstanding the reluctancy of our nature, rectify our tempers and purify our hearts. We must bring "into captivity every thought to the obedience of CHRIST." We must, notwithstanding the allurements of the world, raise our affections to things above, and acquire a relish for spiritual enjoyments. For "without holiness no man shall see the LORD."

Review now the scene of life, and observe how much you have to execute. Consider first what society requires, and then what Religion demands of you.

Confider how great is the work to fulfil our temporal engagements, and to difcharge properly the duties of our ftations. But how much greater ftill, to adorn our profeffion, to perfect holinefs, and to make our calling and election fure! Thefe confiderations might well render us cautious and careful, diligent and expeditious in our work, though we had ever fo large a portion of time allotted us for the performance of it. But, I am now in the

Third place to remind you, that for all our works, even the important work of our falvation, we have but a *day*, that is, only a *fhort* time allowed us; after which " the " night cometh, when no man can work." That our whole life is comparatively but a day; and that a long night will quickly fucceed—are truths that need no proof.

Time

Time rolls on apace, and will soon bring us to our end. In our earliest moments there is but a step between us and death. How many has it surprised in their vigour and strength? Or if we are suffered here to dwell to Nature's utmost limit, how short our stay! And yet, no sooner will this short life be closed, but a period comes to all such working, as will be available to everlasting salvation. Death concludes our trial, and seals our accounts for the day of judgment; when every man shall receive from the LORD " according to that he hath done, whether it be good or evil."

If then we have so much work to perform and such accounts to give; if so much depends upon doing it well, and being able to render a good account; ought we not to apply ourselves to it without delay, and

and to prosecute it with all our vigour? Ought we not to seize the present opportunity, and make the most of the time that lies before us? Is not the work worthy our attention, and shall we not be rewarded for all our pains? Shall the low affairs and empty delights of this world raise our passions and stimulate our powers to perpetual action, and shall we be sluggish and languid in the concerns of the other, where we ought to be most vigilant, industrious and unwearied? Shall we strive so much for the things on earth, and shall heaven and eternity be unregarded? consider I beseech you—suppose you should gain the whole world, what amends will it make for the loss of your souls? And yet your souls you must lose, if you work not the works of him that sent you. You design perhaps to do it at some future opportunity. But if you defer it to day, who will secure to you

the

the morrow? This night, for aught you know, your fouls may be required of you. And fhould they be required, what becomes of our intended penitents? Will their intention of being good hereafter, fave them? Will not their obftinacy in rejecting fo many calls utterly confound and condemn them? Their projected righteoufnefs can be of no avail. " In the trefpaffes they had trefpaffed, and in the fins they had finned *in them* they died," and *for them* they fhall be judged.

But fuppofe our departure fhould not be fo fudden; fuppofe life fhould be continued to us; yet, if we idly neglect the prefent opportunities of well-doing, how are we fure that we fhall ever meet with any more? Or if we *do*, yet what fecurity have we that they fhall prove equal to thofe we now enjoy? Perhaps, they may neither be

fo

so many, nor so advantageous. For the further we enter into the pursuits of this life, the fewer opportunities we shall have of course to mind our spiritual concerns. And the further we advance in years, the less able we shall be, in all probability, to make a right use of those that offer. The day of health is often much shorter than that of animal life: and when sickness comes, what service can we perform to any purpose? How shall we be able to exert ourselves when languor and sorrow have depressed our spirits? This is a reflection of great moment; and of which therefore we are frequently reminded. And did we seriously lay it to heart, surely we should remember our Creator betimes; and finish his works before the evil days come, and the years draw nigh, when we can neither do any service, nor enjoy any comfort.

And

And we have still the more reason to be thus early and careful in our application, because there is an accepted time, a day of salvation; which may be closed before the close of life, or even the loss of natural abilities. We have strong intimations given us, that GOD has fixed a time wherein he expects our repentance and amendment, and beyond which no grace or favour will be found. Not that sincere repentance and real amendment will ever come too late for acceptance. " When " the wicked man turneth away from his " wickedness that he hath committed, and doeth that which is lawful and right;" we may pronounce upon the highest authority, that " he shall save his soul alive." But we have no authority to pronounce, that they may at pleasure do good, who have been accustomed to do evil: or, that such as have long been sinning wilfully,

shall

shall immediately be capable of repentance, on their vouchsafing to cast some thoughts that way. If we reason from similar cases we shall be led to a very different conclusion. We see almost daily examples, wherein mere sorrow, and even ardent wishes, nay, real endeavours are found insufficient to repair a man's fortune, or to restore his health, when he has wasted and destroyed them by extravagance and riot. And, if such methods are thus unable to set all right in men's temporal concerns; what wise man would reduce himself to a necessity of trying their success in an affair of infinitely greater moment—reduce himself to the necessity of relying on their efficacy, not only for removing the dreadful consequences of a life of sin, but for securing the rewards of a life of holiness? The truth is, that repentance itself is no such easy matter as seems to be too commonly supposed.

The

## SERMON VII.

The completion of it at leaft, if not the firft motion towards it, is certainly the gift of God. And how can the habitual finner prefume, that the fpirit of God fhould always counfel him? Why fhould he not rather apprehend, that the time may foon come, when, though he fhould be willing to inherit the blefling he hath profanely defpifed, his pretenfions fhall be rejected? —not becaufe real repentance would even then be unavailable, fuppofing him capable of it; but becaufe he will then have loft the power, the poffibility of repentance.

Hear now the conclufion of the whole—the application that we fhould make of this important fubject. We are fent into the world by our great Creator upon a fervice of infinite confequence, to be accomplifhed, if at all, in this our day. With many of us the day is already far spent, and the night is at hand: it therefore behoves us to examine our progress. Have we carefully attended to the work of our salvation? Have we honestly pursued the business of our stations? Have we been studuious to adorn our Christian profession? Have we laboured to avoid every vice, and to improve in every virtue? Have we observed the statutes and ordinances of the Lord—been constant in our private and public devotions—and more especially in our attendance at the altar? Have we behaved in all the relations of life suitably to the obligations that lay upon us? Have we shewed the love of GOD ingrafted in our hearts, and made his glory the end of our actions? If we have; then are we true and faithful servants; and may expect hereafter to be blessed in our deeds. But if we have not; then, believe me, it is high time we should look to ourselves, and not only think upon, but instantly practise all these things. For *our* obligations to the practice of goodness are peculiarly strong; and our deficiences in this respect will be proportionably punished. Remember, we have been hired in the morning, taken into the vineyard in the beginning of life—have engaged with our master to work there—have had many advantages to forward our labour:—shall *we* then, regardless of these engagements, stand here all the day idle, or, which is worse than idleness, employ ourselves in the service of sin? We do it at our peril—at the peril of our souls—at the peril of eternal destruction to our souls and bodies in another state. We *die* indeed; but what then? Shall we not rise again into another life, where our situation will be determined by our present conduct? As sure as it is appointed us once to die, fo after *that* there will be a judgment; when he who knew his Lord's will, and prepared not himfelf, neither did according to his will, fhall fuffer grievous condemnation.

Since, therefore, death puts an end to our trial, and configns us to our eternal doom; let us think betimes, how dreadful the approach of it muft appear, fhould the bufinefs of our lives ftand *then* unfinifhed! In *early* years indeed, while the circulations are free, and the fpirits lively, time may glide along with tolerable fmoothnefs in a courfe of unthinking gaiety. The *young* man may rejoice in his youth, and let his heart cheer him. He may for fome time walk in his own ways, and follow his own devices, indulging himfelf without referve in the gratification of every fenfe and of every appetite. But, when he comes to be be chilled by age,—the voice of the Lord will be heard in that cool of his day. And, when the remonstrances of conscience begin to upbraid him, what must be the searchings of his heart! What must be the agonies of his soul, when he finds himself obliged to leave this world, having scarcely done any work for which he was sent into it; and is just entering into another—poor and naked, without having provided any requisite qualification for it;—that other, in which he knows, that for the short pleasures of this life there await him endless torments. Such is the end of vanity and folly.

As for the righteous it is not so with him. He has quite another prospect. In the evening of life he can look back with pleasure on the scene that is past; for each part affords him comfort. His work is done;

done; and he waits with serenity for the coming of his master;—in humble confidence that " his reward is with him, and " his works before him." When he enters into the valley of the shadow of death, he will fear no evil; for he knows that his Redeemer liveth, and that he shall live also. And when he is risen into that *other* life, he will assuredly find that his labour in *this* was not in vain. The Lord has prepared a place for him; and will receive him with that high approbation, " Well " done, thou good and faithful servant; " thou hast been faithful over a few things, " I will make thee ruler over many things: " enter thou into the joy of thy Lord."

That we may *all* obtain this approbation, and be at last admitted into that state of glory, let us apply ourselves to God for guidance and support through this

this arduous undertaking. Let us humbly befeech Him, that he would turn away our eyes left they behold wickednefs, and quicken us in his way. That he would infpire us with refolution, and ftrengthen us with might for the tafk affigned us. That he would give us grace, as to begin, fo to go on, continually abounding in the work of the Lord through the day of life; for the night of death will quickly overtake us, when we can no longer work.

# SERMON VIII.

# SERMON VIII.

### EPHESIANS vi. 4.

#### BRING THEM UP IN THE NURTURE AND ADMONITION OF THE LORD.

THE goodnefs of God is in no inftance more difcernible than in providing againft the infirmities of our helplefs ftate, and providing for our welfare from our earlieft infancy. When we come into the world we find, that his providence, attentive to our various wants, has kindly made all proper provifion both for our prefent and future

## SERMON VIII.

future happiness. He has laid our parents under the strongest injunctions to support, cherish and take care of us—and has implanted in their constitutions, a vigorous and lively affection, to urge them to the observance of this necessary duty.

Under the influence of this affection, the duty is indeed in some degree observed, and we feel in proportion the advantages, which arise from the exercise of it. But, notwithstanding the duty is generally acknowledged, and as generally practised after a certain rate; yet the true and proper method of discharging it is neither duly considered nor attended to. Parents, mistaken in their estimate of things, frequently lay the greatest stress on comparatively small and trivial matters. Enamoured of the world themselves, and observing the value that is set upon it by others, they are

are too apt to confine their views to this temporal fcene of things; and fondly to imagine, that they are then confulting the chief and moft valuable intereft of their offspring, when they employ their care to fettle them creditably, as they conceive, in life; and to form them to thofe habits, manners and difpofitions, which are thought anfwerable to their intended ftations. And indeed, confidered as beings deftined to act a part in the world, children do certainly ftand in need of fuch care to fet them out; and of fuch inftructions to render them equal to their future occupations. But then it fhould be remembered, that, as this world is connected with another; and the employments and tranfactions of he prefent life, will hereafter influence our eternal condition; fo the principles upon which they are performed, and the manner in which they are conducted,
fhould

should be conformable—not with the maxims of worldly wisdom, but with those rules of piety and virtue, which GOD has delivered for the security of our present and future happiness. In this view religion, as it contains those rules, appears of the utmost importance; and justly claims our principal regard in the management and education of children. For if they are not impressed with right principles at first, and "train'd up in the way they should go;" they will of course imbibe wrong principles, and be seduced into the way they should not go. And hence it is, that the scripture, aware of the danger they run, is so pressing with us, not to leave them to themselves and the world, to pick up their notions and practice, as casual conversation or example may suggest; but to train them up under such discipline and instruction, as may lead them to the knowledge of

## SERMON VIII.

of the Religion of Christ; and moſt effectually diſpoſe them to profeſs and practiſe it. "Bring them up," ſays the Apoſtle, "in the nurture and admonition of "the Lord." And, ſince ſo much depends on the due performance of this duty—on bringing up children in the manner here ſpecified, I ſhall therefore endeavour, as my ſubject requires, to inform you, in the

Firſt place, wherein this duty conſiſts, and how it ought to be performed.

And then, ſecondly, lay before you ſuch arguments and motives as may incite you to perform and diſcharge it accordingly.

Now, the firſt thing enjoined on parents by this command, is—to cauſe their children to learn in their infancy the doctrines and

and precepts of Religion. The minds of children are not only so tender as to be capable of receiving any impressions; but they are likewise so formed, that they must necessarily receive some. What kind of impressions those are, which they first receive, is a point of the highest consequence. For those first impressions generally sink very deep; and have a lasting influence on their growing lives. Upon which account, it should be the parent's chief concern to give piety and virtue the first possession of their hearts. To this end, they should, from the beginning, be taught to know the God who made them; and to acknowledge that providence, which continually supports them.— They should, from the earliest dawn of reason, be directed to the Lord that bought them; and to that Holy Spirit whose office it is to sanctify them:—and so be led on to those other branches

## SERMON VIII.

branches of knowledge, which are neceſſary to make us wife unto ſalvation. As their minds open, theſe things ſhould be explained to them; and their weight and importance often preſſed and inculcated upon them. Neglect them not at this favourable ſeaſon: for they themſelves invite you to the work, by the curioſity which they diſcover to be acquainted with things, and the attention which they give to information. Pour your leſſons gradually into them, as they are able to comprehend them—line upon line, and precept upon precept—that their improvement in knowledge may keep pace with their ſtature, and their piety riſe in proportion to their years.

All parents indeed are not, I grant, equally qualified for this undertaking, ſo as to perform it in a maſterly way. Moſt of them however, if not all, might, did they

they choose, by the help of that compendious catechism which the church has provided, convey to their children sufficient instruction, and that in a proper and effectual method, with respect to the most needful and necessary truths. And it behoves them to reflect, that they will be utterly inexcusable, if they do not faithfully instil into their minds those first principles of our holy Religion, with which they are so readily and easily furnished:— if they do not instruct them in the nature and obligation of the christian covenant— what mercies are offered on God's part, and what duties are required on theirs— what they are to believe, and what they are to do, in order to be saved.

When this foundation is laid, you must then refer them to the holy scriptures—a portion of which they should daily read—

and

and oblige them, at the same time, to a regular attendance on public discourses for further improvement in religious knowledge. By these means they will be so rooted and grounded in the truth, as to be able to withstand the opposing blasts of false doctrine; and to confute the cunning sophistry of those, who may attempt to seduce them into error.

This is one point gained: but when this is gained, you are by no means to stop here. For after they are instructed in the *knowledge* of their duty, they should also be brought up in the constant *practice* and *observance* of it. They must not only be taught to know God, but they must likewise be accustomed to worship him. They must not only be made sensible of the reasonableness and excellency of the divine commands; but they must likewise be habituated to pay a due and proper regard to them. If children are early accuftomed to addrefs themfelves to GOD, and to approach him with that reverence both in public and private, which is fuitable to the majefty of Heaven and earth; it will raife in them an awful fenfe of the Deity, and render them obfervant of what he enjoins. The obfervance of his laws, perfifted in for a time, will give them a bias on the fide of virtue; and gradually confirm them in well-doing. *This* the apoftle plainly faw muft be the natural confequence of fuch good beginnings; and therefore *this* is what he principally recommends to the care and attention of parents. For he exhorts them not merely to *inftruct*, but to " *bring*" or *train* up their children " in the nurture and admonition of the " LORD:" that is, not only to *teach* them fome truths, neceffary to be known or believed,

lieved, but to endeavour to form thofe truths into *practical principles*, fo as to render them of habitual good influence on their temper and conduct, in the various occurrences of life.

" Doubtlefs Religion requires inftruction; for it depends on our knowing and believing fome truths: and fo does common prudence in temporal affairs depend on our knowing others. Yet neither of them confift in the bare knowledge or belief of thofe truths; but in our being brought by fuch knowledge or belief to a correfpondent temper and behaviour. Religion, as it ftood under the Old Teftament, is perpetually called the Fear of GOD; under the New, Faith in CHRIST. Now, as that fear of GOD does not fignify literally—being afraid of him, but having a good heart, and leading a good life, in confequence of that fear;

so this faith in CHRIST does not signify literally being convinced that he is the Messiah, but the becoming his real disciples, and fulfilling his commands, in consequence of such conviction."

Our Religion then being thus *practical*, consisting in a frame of mind and course of behaviour, suitable to the commands of GOD, and conducive to our final happiness; children ought, by education, to be led on to this course of behaviour, and formed into this frame and disposition of mind. And it deserves our consideration, that if no care be taken to do it, they will grow up in a directly contrary behaviour, and be hardened in directly contrary habits. Of this indeed we are sufficiently sensible, as far as relates to those outward ornaments which are necessary to fit them for the converse of the world. And therefore, instead

of

of leaving them to themselves, we provide masters to instruct them in every graceful and polite accomplishment. In the performance of which, we do not only expect that they should lay before them the rules of their art, but that they should likewise superintend, conduct and guide them in the practice and exercise of those rules; without which they would remain as destitute of those several accomplishments, as if they had never been taught. But if so much care and pains be requisite to fashion the outward man to all the graces and elegance of motion; can we ever suppose that the inward man can be formed by less to the more difficult rules of virtue? And yet, how little care do we properly apply to this needful purpose? *Who* think of making it their business, though really it is the business of all, to regulate the wills, to govern the passions, and to direct the affections of their children? Are not the reins generally thrown loose upon their necks for several years together; and they allowed to do just what is right in their own eyes? Or, if we confine them, for the sake of saving appearances, to the modes and forms of external decorum, yet how seldom do we attempt to correct the internal depravity and perverseness of their hearts? And therefore what wonder, if, when they are grown to maturer years, they should, notwithstanding the profession of Christianity, exert all the passions of undisciplined nature, and run counter to every thing that is virtuous and good!

Now, in order to secure them from this extreme, be careful to inspect their natural dispositions. See where their greatest danger lies: observe which is their weakest side: and then endeavour all you can to for-

## SERMON VIII. 167

fortify by art, what is thus left unguarded by nature. Call in all poffible affiftance: implore the divine grace for their improvement; and inftruct them to do the fame. Inculcate upon them all thofe virtues, which are moft agreeable to their condition; and cautioufly reftrain them from thofe vices, to which they are addicted by the inexperience of their years, or the bias of their inclinations. Shew them particularly the amiablenefs of Religion in your own lives; and let them fee by your converfation, how lovely a thing it is to be good. Example is, with all, far more prevalent than precept; and efpecially with children, who are remarkably prone to imitate. This then fhould induce you to keep a conftant guard upon your conduct; and not only to abftain from grofs fins before them, but even to avoid all fuch practices as have the leaft tendency to what is evil. For though you should give them the most perfect instructions—should tell them of the folly of such and such indulgences, the vanity of such and such pursuits, and the sinfulness of such and such actions; yet, if they observe you indulging in the things you condemned, pursuing the things you judged vain, and acting the part you pronounced sinful; what can you expect but that their passions should be excited by what you do; and that they should consequently be prompted to follow you into the same excess of sin and riot. Therefore, as you value their welfare, keep a strict guard upon your words and actions: do nothing before them, but what they may safely copy: let your example be their guide: and whenever they chance to deviate from the right, temper your correction to their genius and dispositions. The better to encourage you to this care, I come now, in the

Second

## SERMON VIII.

Second place, to point out some of those great advantages, that would naturally flow from thence, as well to yourselves, as to your children. And with regard to the children, such an education will put them in the way of securing both their temporal and eternal interest. For " Godliness is " profitable unto all things; having the " promise of the life that now is, as well " as of that which is to come." It is the safest guide to what is good; and the greatest preservative against evil. It will teach them the truest enjoyment of what this world affords; and crown them at last with endless felicity in the other. And with regard to the parents, the happy effect of their care will be, that they will reap the comfort, and certainly great comfort it is, of seeing their children rising into life under a promising aspect—then acting, in every station, just as becomes them—and passing
through

through the world with efteem and approbation. Sons or daughters, thus wife and thus virtuous, will make their fathers glad. And among their other virtues, that filial affection, which in a good perfon is moft vigorous towards an aged parent, will adminifter fuch joy to their decaying life, as no one can conceive, but they who feel it. Such is generally the bleffed fruit of an early piety. But, if their children fhould, as they fometimes may, prove the reverfe of all this, and turn out undutiful and wicked; yet the parents will extract this confolation from it—that they have nothing to reproach themfelves withal; but have done every thing that in them lay, to guard againft and prevent it. Whereas, in the other cafe, when they are neglected in their younger years, and fuffered to proceed according to the bent of their own inclinations, as they will neceffarily become

come bad in all relations, so the guilt of all their sins will, in a great measure, be chargeable on those, whose duty it was to have taught them better. Nay, it will extend further;—even to the sins of their children's children. For, as by training up your own offspring in the ways of Religion, you may be laying instruction for their posterity, to the increase and improvement of your future reward; so by being careless of them you may ruin their descendants for many generations, to the aggravation of your future punishment. Nor imagine, that the wrong habits, which they have early contracted through your neglect, should ever be corrected afterwards. For if children set out at first in a wrong way, they generally continue the same erroneous track all their lives. They are commonly hurried into the world so soon,

soon, and then so busily engaged in it, that they will not give themselves time to reflect and consider; or if they did, have not the faculties perhaps to reason themselves into virtue. Of this we have daily proofs that should make us tremble.

We are apt to complain, that the present age is loose and wicked. And were any one to take a religious survey of these great cities—the general decay of public piety, much too apparent in our churches on the LORD's day—the profane language and indecency in our streets—with the many other overflowings of ungodliness, would soon convince him that we do not complain without reason. Nevertheless, whenever we condemn the age as bad we should seriously consider, whether we have done *our* part to make it better. Perhaps we we may think, and juftly too, that, with all our endeavours, we fhall be able to gain but little upon thofe, who have been long habituated to a vicious courfe, and are not fubject to our authority. The rifing generation is however in our hands, and we may now model it to what we pleafe. If we faithfully difcharge our duty, and exert a due charity for the fouls intrufted with us, we fhall thereby cover, I mean, *prevent*, a multitude of future fins: But, if we are regardlefs of thefe matters, a heavy charge will lie againft us, and generations yet to come will have juft caufe to deplore our negligence. However harfh this may feem, Truth calls upon me to declare it. I would fain, if it be poffible, awaken parents into a fenfe of their duty; and therefore am bound to fet before them both the terrors and mercies of the LORD; intending by each to

per-

persuade them to become so wise in time, as to serve the Lord with their whole house; training up their families in the way they should go, that it may be well with them, and with their children for ever.

# SERMON IX.

# SERMON IX.

2 PETER iii.—18.

GROW IN GRACE, AND IN THE KNOWLEDGE OF OUR LORD AND SAVIOUR JESUS CHRIST.

IT was, we find, in former times; and it is, we know, in times prefent; a very common miftake among Chriftians—when they have gained fome knowledge of the doctrines of Religion, and made fome advancement in the practice of its duties—

to imagine themselves sufficiently wife, and sufficiently virtuous: and in consequence of that imagination, to rest satisfied with their present attainments, regardless of any further improvements. Now, it is something, to be sure, to understand the principles of the doctrine of Christ, and to be able to give a reason of the hope that is in us; it is something to have laid the foundation of repentance from dead works, and to have made some progress in the ways of righteousness: But, certainly, all this comes far short of the measure of our obligation, and the extent of our duty:—far short of that exalted goodness, which the example of our Saviour recommends, and which the Gospel enjoins as necessary to Salvation. For if we would obtain the prize of our calling—would secure our everlasting inheritance—we must, by no means, content ourselves with

## SERMON IX.

with partial obedience and low proficiencies; but should press on, with vigour, towards perfection—should advance from faith to faith, and proceed from virtue to virtue: exerting all our diligence to " grow *daily* in grace ; and in the knowledge of our Lord and Saviour Jesus Christ."

That you may, then, the better understand the true import, and full meaning of this admonition, and may be the better qualified and disposed to observe it, I shall consider,

First, what it is to grow in grace, and the knowledge of Christ.

Secondly, what necessity there is for aspiring after such growth, and making such improvement. And

Thirdly, by what means such growth and improvement may be made and promoted.

First

First then, since all holy desires, all good resolutions, and all just works, are derived from heaven—from the *gracious* influence of the divine Spirit; therefore the Scripture frequently represents all such desires, resolutions, and actions, by the general name of *grace*. It does so in this place. For to grow in grace, is evidently to grow in all the virtues and graces of a Christian life; that is, to live daily in a more exact and perfect conformity with the rules of the Gospel. But before we can grow to this excellency of practice—this conformity with the rules of the Gospel—we must previously grow in the knowledge of those rules, as there delivered by our Lord and Saviour Jesus Christ. For knowledge is the foundation of practice: and it is impossible for us to obey the will of God, unless we understand what his will is.

The

The firft ftep therefore, in our compliance with the exhortation here given us, muft be—carefully to learn, what it is that the Lord requires of us; in what manner we are to proceed; and how far we are to go. The commandment of God is extremely exact, and, at the fame time, exceedingly broad. It comprehends a large extent, and enjoins a critical precifenefs, of action. This extent of duty, this propriety of action, we fhould carefully examine and ftudioufly adjuft; examine through every part, and adjuft to every circumftance; or otherwife, we may chance to fall into grievous miftakes, and finally perifh in our errors.

But it is not enough that we *know* thefe things; therefore what we have thus learned, we muft, next, endeavour to put in practice. And in this endeavour, as we are sure to be opposed by the strong current of our corrupt inclinations, we must consequently strive to correct our affections—to regulate our passions—and to reduce every licentious imagination to the discipline of Christ. But, thus to rectify the perverseness of our corruption, is a work of no small difficulty. It will require our constant attention, and most vigorous application: nay, though we attend ever so closely, and apply ever so vigorously, yet we may often deviate into sin: but still, if we persevere with patience, we shall gain, in time, frequent victories over ourselves; and make, by degrees, considerable advances in virtue. Whatever virtues we have thus attained, we must make it our business daily to exercise: by such exercise, we shall not only perfect ourselves in those we possess; but shall be led to the acquirement of others. For the

the virtues being all connected together, every one of them is a step or introduction to another. By these steps then, we should continually advance in the ways of piety—ever thankful for every improvement, yet ever ambitious of further progress. For be our improvements what they may, we have no reason, in any part of our lives, to esteem ourselves sufficiently perfect; but, " forgetting those things " that are behind"—laying no stress on those virtues already acquired—" we should " reach forth to those things that are " before," and earnestly aspire to those graces, of which, as yet, we are not possessors. But this will appear more clearly, when I have shewed, in the

Second place, the great necessity of such continued growth, and constant improvement. Though, to persons rightly disposed,

posed, what occasion is there to shew it at all? Needs the man who is sincerely good be told of the necessity of growing better? Will not the same motives that induced him, at first, to enter on a virtuous course, engage him afterwards to persevere in it? —will not the growing easiness allure his steps, and the rising pleasure encourage his progress? But if, either the indolence of his temper should prompt him to remit his care, or the error of the wicked should seduce him from his steadfastness; then let him consider,

That the commandments of GOD strictly enjoin us, as to begin, so to go on in well-doing—to walk worthy of the LORD, and endeavour to be pure like him; being fruitful in every good work—perfecting holiness in his sight.

And

And as the commandments of God *oblige* us to this growth and excellence, so doth his providence graciously *administer* proper opportunities for it. Every day of our lives opens the door to higher attainments; and every circumstance of our condition, rightly used, helps to carry us upwards. It behoves us, then, in the reason of things, to attend diligently to our trust; and make a right use of our talents: to employ every opportunity in the exercise of some virtuous act; and to improve every incident that befalls us to the heightening of some virtuous affection. Much depends upon our so doing. For though God designed us all for happiness, yet has he left us— every man—to work it out for himself. It *can* only be worked out in the way of virtue; and will be proportionable to the progress and diligence we have used in that way. If we are faithful in the discharge of of our duties, we shall accordingly be happy in the enjoyment of ourselves: but, if we should ever abate of our industry, we shall instantly check and damp our felicity. Well then may we dread to lose a day. For in the loss of that day's virtues, may be lost, we know not, how many comforts. In the present state, self-improvement is absolutely necessary to self-enjoyment. We hear of men who daily complain, that their lives are dull and insipid. But how can they be otherwise, when we know, they are so extremely insignificant? Let us be doing good, and, depend upon it, we shall never be dull. Let us add to the day a virtue, and the night will certainly bring us joy. And in what night might we not rejoice, when in any day we may be good? Did we look no further than this present life, it would be greatly our interest, not only to be steadfast and immoveable, but,

to

to be always abounding in the work of the LORD. Such a conduct would secure us from numberless evils; and those it could not prevent, it would enable us cheerfully to support; it would increase the relish of all outward enjoyments; and when those failed, would satisfy us from ourselves. This is no mean recommendation of piety. But the profitableness of it is much greater as it respects another life. The design of religion is to form and dispose us for the reception of those good things, which GOD has prepared for them that love him. And therefore, the more observant we are of its precepts, the better fitted are we to enjoy its promises: and the higher we advance in grace here, the brighter we shall shine in glory hereafter. Hence then, we see the importance of every kind of virtue, and of every degree of goodness.—They are attended —always attended—with proportionable

portionable degrees of happinefs; of happinefs improving to all eternity. And if this be the cafe, as it certainly is, how earneftly fhould we covet the moft excellent gifts; and how ardently fhould we afpire to the moft eminent attainments? To ftop fhort of any attainable degree of virtue, is to deprive ourfelves of a correfponding increafe of happinefs: nay, it is not only to deprive ourfelves of all the happinefs immediately refulting from that degree of virtue, but from all the fubfequent increafe of its eternally growing product.

Some, perhaps, lefs ambitious of fuch an exceeding weight of glory, would reft content with that meafure of holinefs, which is juft fufficient to admit them to heaven. But, then I would afk them, or rather perfuade them to afk themfelves, how do they know, *when* they are poffeffed of

## SERMON IX.

of that neceffary meafure? or indeed, *what that neceffary meafure is?* Different attainments in piety, under different circumftances, will without doubt, carry different perfons to heaven; yet no perfon can have any fecurity, that he fhall there arrive at the loweft, who does not fincerely aim at the higheft happinefs. It is the fincerity of our endeavours that gives them all their value; and there is reafon to think that our hearts are not right—and that we ceafe to be fincere, when we ceafe to aim at the utmoft poffible perfection. Befides,

It is obfervable both of the endowments of grace, and the abilities of nature, that unlefs they are exercifed and improved, they languifh and decay. And therefore, fhould we fuppofe that our good difpofitions are, at prefent, fo ftrong; and our ftock stock of virtue so great, as to entitle us to a high station in the joys of futurity; yet, whenever we leave off increasing our store, and improving our habits, we are in danger of losing the things we had gained; and failing, at last, of our full reward.

Since then the only way to make our calling and election sure, is, to grow daily in grace, and to improve daily in virtue; let us now consider, in the

Third place, by what means such improvement may be made, and such growth promoted.

And the first that recommends itself to us, is the frequent and serious perusal of the holy Scriptures: for these will make us wise unto salvation—instruct us in the nature and extent of our duty; lay before us

## SERMON IX. 191

us the moſt powerful motives of obedience; and engage our compliance by the moſt alluring examples.

Being thoroughly enlightened, directed and encouraged unto all good works; our next care ſhould be, to apply to GOD, in the offices of religion, for ſtrength and power to perform them. We are not able, of ourſelves, to do any thing, as of ourſelves; and therefore ſtand in abſolute need of ſupernatural aſſiſtance. Such requiſite aid GOD is always ready to impart, if we faithfully ſeek it in the way of his ordinances. For theſe ordinances were eſtabliſhed on purpoſe—to fit and prepare us for the grace and influence of the HOLY SPIRIT—and when ſo fitted and prepared, to convey and bring down his grace and influence upon us. By the uſe of theſe means we ſhall find ourſelves ſtrengthened

with

with might in the inner man; and rendered equal to the difficulties of our duty. But to engage this help, and secure this affiftance of the Spirit, we muft be fure to follow his motions, and to concur with his operations. And if we become fellow-workers with him, we fhall, at laft, be conquerors through him.

It concerns us therefore frequently to review our lives, and clofely to examine our conduct—to fee, whether we employ every opportunity, and improve every grace to the purpofes of virtue and goodnefs. Without this, it is impoffible for us, to know our real ftate and condition; and unlefs we know our condition, we can never be anxious to improve it. Let us then firmly refolve to call ourfelves daily to account; and faithfully to adjuft the concerns of our fouls. If upon fuch a retrofpect spect and examination, we find ourselves backward in our Christian course; and low in spiritual attainments: if we find ourselves either so clogged by the cares, entangled in the pleasures, or oppressed by the troubles of the world, that we cannot rise to any considerable heights in piety; then,

Let us reflect, in the last place, that as this is the thing to which we are called, the only thing needful; so it is the only thing that deserves our attention, and is worth our pains. When we labour for the things of this world, we labour for shadows and short-lived vanities; but whilst we are labouring for christian perfection, we are labouring for eternity, and securing to ourselves a solid, never-ending happiness. Whatever enjoyments the world may propose, let us consider—that the world and all

its enjoyments muſt ſhortly have an end.
" The laſt hour will ſoon be with us, when
" we ſhall have nothing to look for, but
" our reward in another life ;—when we
" ſhall ſtand with nothing but eternity
" before us ;—and muſt begin to be ſome-
" thing—that will be our ſtate for ever.
" Let us then provide againſt this impor-
" tant hour, and look out, in time, for
" comfort. Let us treaſure up ſuch a fund
" of good works as may enable us to bear
" that ſtate, which cannot be borne with-
" out them." But ſuch works—ſuch good
works—will not only enable us to bear,
but alſo to enjoy, that future ſtate. For
the more perfect we make ourſelves here,
the more happy we ſhall be hereafter.
And is not this, let me aſk you, a conſideration ſufficient in reaſon to excite the
moſt languid to aſpire with earneſtneſs to
every improvement in Piety and Virtue?
And

And who, that truly afpires to them, may not effectually attain them? In this life, though we labour ever fo hard, we may not, with all our pains, either acquire any confiderable enjoyments, or rife to any confiderable eminence. But in the other life, our ftation may be as high, and our condition as happy, as ever we pleafe to make them. All the glories of heaven, and all the joys at God's right hand, lie open to us—invite our purfuit—and will reward our fidelity. Having then, my brethren, an entrance adminiftered into fuch a glorious ftate, let us do all we can to gain admittance. Strait indeed is the gate, and narrow is the way that leadeth into this blisful life; yet, if we labour and ftrive, we may be in the number of thofe who pafs it. And when we are entered in, we fhall find that our labour was not in vain: for, we fhall find an happinefs provided for us—full as our wifhes, everlafting as our fouls.

# SERMON X.

# SERMON X.

### EXODUS 20.—8.

REMEMBER THE SABBATH-DAY, TO KEEP IT HOLY.

THIS is one of the ten commandments, which GOD delivered to the Israelites from mount Sinai: or rather, it is the re-injunction of a command, which he had before given to ADAM at the beginning of the world. For, in the history of the creation, written by MOSES, it is said—that " GOD blessed the seventh day, and sancti-
" fied

"fied it:" that is, set it apart—as a day of rest from bodily labour, and a day to be employed in holy and religious acts—in admiring the glories of the new-raised fabrick of the world, and adoring the perfections of its excellent architect.

This first sabbath indeed, our original parents must, by the very emotions of nature, have been induced to celebrate, though there had been no command. Created, as they were, at the close of the sixth day, they did, of course, begin the seventh with the contemplation of the world around them: and when they beheld so much power, wisdom and goodness, displayed through the whole, and supereminently exemplified in themselves; they could not fail to give thanks unto the LORD with their whole hearts, and to speak of all his marvellous works.

But

But how lively foever thefe grateful impreffions might have been, and how warmly foever, in confequence of thofe impreffions, their devotion might flow, at firft; yet, a little time, without fomething to revive them, would have cooled the one, and effaced the other. An uninterrupted converfe with the objects of fenfe, and a clofe application to the purfuits of life, muft neceffarily have diverted their attention, and withdrawn their regard, from the things pertaining to God. To break the force of fuch worldly attachment, and to keep alive a fenfe of religion, one day in every feven was, from the beginning, appointed to be kept holy unto the Lord, and to be employed in his worfhip and fervice.

But if fuch an inftitution were neceffary to preferve in the minds of our firft parents the remembrance of the creation, and of the

the duties they owed to their great Creator; then the same institution is equally necessary to preserve in the minds of all their children the remembrance of the same truths. The reason of this appointment then, being thus founded in the constitution of human nature, and the appointment itself being equally conducive to the improvement and happiness of all mankind; it clearly follows, that all mankind are equally included under the original command, and equally bound to observe and obey it. From this short account of the institution of the Sabbath, it plainly appears, that it was not merely intended for a day of rest, but also for a day of public worship. Nay, so far is the bare rest, or suspension of labour, from answering the design of the institution, that, with respect to mankind, rest was only therefore commanded, that they might be at leisure to attend the service of God. In

## SERMON X.

In thefe religious fervices, at firft, God was confidered as the Creator and Governour of the world; and the adoration then paid him was chiefly adapted to thofe relations. Some general acknowledgment the faithful, we may fuppofe, did likewife make of their belief in the promifed Messiah; and clofed the whole with thankfgivings for all experienced, and fupplications for all expected, mercies.

In after-times, when the Ifraelites were delivered from the bondage of Egypt, the celebration of the Sabbath was, by the appointment of God himfelf, made the memorial of that deliverance; and the acknowledgment of the divine goodnefs in that fignal mercy was probably fuperadded to the fervice of the day.

But, as this deliverance from Egypt was only

only a prelude to, and a type of our redemption by Christ; the memorial of the type was confequently dropt, when the thing typified was known to be accomplifhed. The Sabbath, indeed, was ftill celebrated; but the time of its celebration was changed. For, as our redemption was finally accomplifhed by our Saviour's rifing from the dead on the firft day of the week, therefore his Apoftles, without departing from the primitive inftitution of one day in feven, made the day of his refurrection the day of affembling for the worfhip of God, both as Creator and Redeemer. And all Chriftians, with as great propriety as unanimity, have obferved the fame ever fince, in imitation of their example.

Thus you perceive for what end the Sabbath was firft appointed, and how it after-

afterwards came to be changed. Though, under all changes, the end was still the fame. And in truth a gracious and wife end it is. For in the road of life, where worldly concerns prefs so thick, and solicit our purfuit with so much importunity; it is impoffible for us to maintain a proper fenfe of Religion, unlefs we retire at ftated times, and apply ourfelves to prayer and meditation. Indeed, as our fouls are fo clofely united to flefh, and fo prone to fink into fenfuality, frequent application to fuch exercifes is no more than fufficient to preferve it. Hence it is much to be feared, that the flame of devotion, which the public fervice of one Sunday may have raifed, will be nearly extinguifhed, if not daily fed, before the next arrives. And if the weekly fervices of the church, with only the intermiffion of fix days' devotion, cannot make the comers thereunto perfect;

fect; how far from Christian perfection must they be, who neglect both public and private devotion!

As this institution then was entirely designed for the security and advancement of our happiness; we are bound by interest as well as duty to shew a due and constant regard to it; or else we shall incur the guilt, not only of disobeying an express command of GOD, but also of defeating one of the most gracious designs that his wisdom could contrive for the good and benefit of our souls.

Now this guilt may be contracted, either by neglecting the LORD's-day, or by profaning it.

The Sabbath is a day to be kept holy to the LORD; that is, to be entirely devoted

to

to his fervice. But the principal part of his fervice is public worſhip. And therefore an habitual abſence from that worſhip is one of the moſt glaring inſtances of the neglect of his day. An inſtance—that proves thoſe who are guilty of it to be equally regardleſs of their own welfare, as of God's honour. For what can be a clearer proof, that men care not to improve in virtue, and conſequently in happineſs, than wilfully to abſent themſelves from that ordinance, which was purpoſely appointed for their improvement? To ſuch, I have nothing more to ſay. To you, whoſe appearance in this place indicates another temper, I would offer the words of congratulation. Herein, however, let us not think of ourſelves more highly than we ought to think. We may appear in this place, and yet, through the want of attentiveneſs and devotion, may be chargeable

able at the fame time with a neglect very little inferior to theirs who never appear at all. For, to be inattentive when prefent, is, in effect, to be abfent. Mere bodily worfhip, to fay the moft of it, is but a fuperficial fhew of Religion. And in this fuperficial way, we may be very punctual in our attendance on the public worfhip all our lives, and yet be never the better Chriftians.

God is a Spirit; and they that worfhip him truly, muft worfhip him in Spirit. But the foul is the only Spiritual part of our compofition; and therefore it is the foul alone that can approach and converfe with a pure Spiritual Being. Nor can we otherwife, through our fouls, make this approach,—otherwife maintain this converfation with him, than by keeping our thoughts fixed upon him. It muft be allowed,

lowed, that to raife our carnal minds to the contemplation of fpiritual things is very difficult; and when raifed, to keep them fixed, much more difficult. But neverthelefs, as the efficacy of our devotion depends upon our attention; we fhould, by all means, endeavour to acquire it. And means there are, which, duly employed, will effectually produce it.

The chief reafon why our thoughts are fo little intent upon GOD, is, that they are too much attached to the world. They are fo entangled in the bufinefs of the week, that a Sunday's retreat cannot difengage them. And therefore the firft ftep towards the attainment of a devout attention, is to moderate our concern for the bufinefs of life, and withdraw our affections from the world.

When the concerns of the world are thus banifhed, and the heart is prepared for the exercife of religion ; that which muft fix our attention, through the feveral parts of divine worfhip, is, a thorough fenfe of the manifold wants we have to be fupplied,— and a thorough conviction, that fincere, warm, lively devotion is the means of obtaining a fupply for them.

Let us but enter on the public worfhip, with a deep and due fenfe of our repeated offences againft God, and of the dreadful confequences thereunto annexed ; and this alone will make us both penitently ferious in the confeffion of thofe offences, and humbly grateful for the declaration that is made of the remiffion of them.

Let us but be convinced of our natural weaknefs and acquired depravity—of our indifindisposition and inability to perform, as we ought, the will of God; and that conviction will, of course, enliven our devotion and communicate a warmth to those addresses we make to him for the supplies of his grace, and the assistance of his Holy Spirit.

Let us but sedately reflect, how frail our constitution is,—to what miseries and dangers we are constantly exposed; and that very reflection will be sufficient to keep us devout and attentive, whenever we implore the aid and protection of Heaven.

Lastly, let us but consider what numberless blessings the divine goodness daily and hourly confers upon us; and our gratitude will engage all the powers of our souls, when we offer up our praises and thanksgivings for them.

These are sure methods, whereby the spirit of prayer may be excited, quickened, and kept alive within us; and which therefore we should be careful to pursue and to improve. Though I must not forget to add, that the consideration of GOD's peculiar presence in our religious assemblies contributes not a little to the same effect; as it induces on our minds a reverential awe, and disposes us to seriousness, gravity, and attention.

I have hitherto insisted only on the constant and devout performance of public worship—as being the most important and necessary part of this day's solemnity. But there are other duties, belonging to it, which, though of a more private nature, should, by no means, be neglected.—Even all the duties, which tend to improve, either in ourselves or others, the knowledge

ledge and practice of Religion. Such are, for inftance—the recollecting, and applying to ourfelves, the good leffons we have learned—reading the holy fcriptures and other pious books — meditating on the works of nature and grace—examining the paft conduct of our lives, and ftating and adjufting the accounts of our fouls—and, if we are parents or mafters, the inftructing thofe who are committed to our care in the principles and duties of Chriftianity; and reftraining them from all fuch actions as are inconfiftent with the facrednefs of a day fet apart for religious purpofes.

What has been already advanced to fhew the finfulnefs of neglecting the LORD's day, is of much greater force to fhew the finfulnefs of profaning it. For this latter makes a large addition of guilt to the former; and renders the fin of neglecting, as the

Apof-

Apostle speaks, exceeding sinful. When the leisure that was designed for improvement in virtue, is made the occasion of increasing in wickedness; when the time that was appointed for the service of GOD, is altogether employed in the service of Satan, the guilt is aggravated to the highest pitch that human corruption is able to raise it.

Instances of such guilt, great as it is, we see, alas! too many. Should they become general, what infinite detriment would it be to the world? And yet, every man, who, on this day, wilfully neglects the service of GOD, is in a ready way to add to their number. For what is the neglect of GOD's worship, but the neglect of that which is the proper culture of the Soul, and which alone can prevent a man from becoming abandoned?

In

# SERMON X.

In the patriarchal times, when religious knowledge was altogether conveyed by oral tradition, and thofe traditions were chiefly delivered in their public affemblies on the Sabbath-days; it is eafy to fee of what great importance a due attendance upon thofe affemblies muft have been. The prefervation of religion in the world evidently depended upon it. And the fpeedy decay of piety, together with the quick growth of immorality, fo juftly remarkable in thofe early times, can be attributed to nothing with fo much probability, as to their neglect of affembling themfelves together—as the manner of fome now is.

But are not thefe confiderations almoft equally applicable to the prefent age? What! Though we live in the bleffed days of a *written* Gofpel, and enjoy it in a language which we all underftand; yet, does not the misfortune of not *knowing letters* reduce many of us to the ignorant ftate of our primitive anceftors? And of thofe who can read the Scriptures, how few, in comparifon, are they who can read them with judgment and profit! Something, to be fure, they will learn from them. They will learn at leaft to be convinced of their own ignorance, and of the great ufe of public inftruction.

Thefe reflections, one would think, fhould have a peculiar influence upon fome people; and yet, what little weight they have with thofe who are moft concerned, is obvious from hence—that they, who, for the fake of gaining inftruction, ought of all men to frequent the church moft, in fact, attend it leaft.

But,

## SERMON X.

But, though I have made the ignorance of the lower fort a peculiar argument for their attendance; thofe in a more exalted fituation, however, muſt in no wife imagine, that their knowledge will excufe their abfence. So far from it, that this very confideration fhould make them conſtant. For they, whom God hath diſtinguiſhed with greater marks of his bounty and favour, are, in gratitude, obliged to diftinguiſh themfelves by greater degrees of public acknowledgment. So that we are, with refpect to this duty, high and low, all upon an equality; equally bound to perform it devoutly, and equally benefited by the performance.

Loud are the complaints—of the depravity of the age. Would we then make it better? Let the reformation begin with the confcientious obfervance of this day.

Sunday well spent will extend its influence through the whole week. Weeks improved will better months—and months, years. It is agreed on all hands, that the virtue and morals of mankind can be improved and supported only by Religion. But what is to support Religion itself? Various indeed are the means that may help towards it; but there is one mean worth them all, and without which all the rest will be ineffectual: this God, in his wisdom has provided for us, and bound upon us—and is no other than the regular observation of his Holy Day.

Since therefore so much depends upon this duty, it becomes every one's concern, as he tenders the honour of God, and the welfare of Religion—as he values his own happiness—the happiness of his family, or the happiness of society—it concerns him,

I say, by example, by authority, by inftruction, by every method in his power, to encourage and promote the practice of it. And was our light fo to fhine—was our regard for Religion fo to appear before men, feveral who are now negligent, feeing our good works, might be induced to tread in our fteps, and follow us to this place to glorify our Father who is in heaven. And in that cafe, how infinitely great would be our comfort here; how infinitely glorious our reward hereafter! For they that turn many to righteoufnefs fhall fhine forth as the ftars for ever and ever.

SERMON

# SERMON XI.

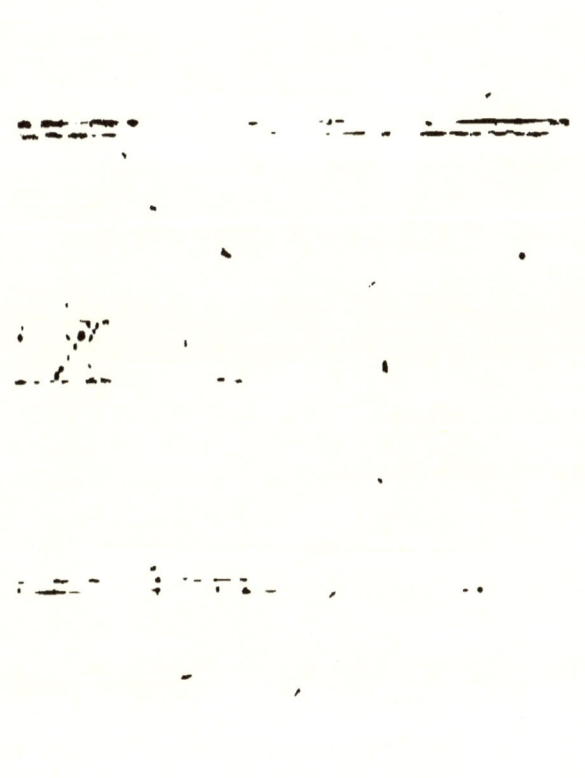

# SERMON XI.

1 PETER iv.—18.

AND IF THE RIGHTEOUS SCARCELY BE SAVED, WHERE SHALL THE UNGODLY AND THE SINNER APPEAR?

THAT christianity is no idle profession,—that the attainment of salvation is no easy undertaking,—must needs, I think, be evident to us, from the laboriousness of those exercises, and the hardships of those em-

employments, with which the fcripture compares it. And yet, if we take a view of the world, and obferve the general conduct of Chriftians, it fhould feem as if they were actuated by another opinion;—as if they thought Religion to be as indulgent, as it is merciful;—as eafy to be practifed, as it is to be profeffed.

For if here and there we fee a few, who, confcious of the neceffity of a good life, follow Righteoufnefs with diligence and affiduity; what an infinite number do we fee befides, who give themfelves up to their bufinefs, or their pleafures, ftrangely regardlefs of that great concern? Our Saviour, it is true, has fmoothed our road, in a wonderful degree, to eternal happinefs; and the Holy Spirit is always ready to affift our progrefs in the way of falvation. But neverthelefs, our road in reality is neither

ther so smooth, nor that progress so easy to be made, as we generally imagine. Great difficulties still remain; and duties, hard to be performed, are required of us: and hence it is, that we are so frequently admonished by our SAVIOUR and his Apostles to *watch*, to *labour*, to *strive*, that we may be able to obtain the end of our calling. But we are no where excited to a careful discharge of our Christian duties by a more powerful argument than what is couched in the words of the text; which equally comprehend both sorts of men in the world:—as well those, who vigorously pursue the means of Salvation; as those, who are remiss, or totally negligent of their duty.

To support and perpetuate the diligence of the former, they are here assured, that all their endeavours are but just sufficient.

And to confound and quaſh the vain hopes of the latter, they are given to underſtand, that the Righteous with all their care are ſcarcely ſaved : and conſequently, that their own condition muſt be dreadful, and full of danger. For " if the righteous be ſcarcely " ſaved, where ſhall the ungodly and the " ſinner appear ?"

To enforce this conſideration upon each ſort of men, is the great deſign of theſe alarming words ; whoſe import, that they may the better obtain their effect, I am now going to ſet before you.

The Apoſtle here affirms, that even the Righteous is ſcarcely ſaved. Not that he would be thought to mean, that the Righteous ſhall *not* be ſaved ; for he that feareth God and keepeth his commandments, is, through the merits of Christ, ſecure of Sal-

Salvation by the Gospel-covenant: but his meaning is, that the Religion, which by this covenant we engage to observe, and the service we are obliged to perform, is a work of great difficulty; and requires no less, than the constant labour of our whole lives, to be discharged in a proper manner. The Righteous shall certainly be saved: but then, the Christian character of a Righteous man implies much more than the world commonly annexes to it. It is not merely to be chaste and temperate—it is not merely to be just or generous—it is not merely to be devout and charitable: in short, it is not to abstain from this or that vice, and to practise this or the other virtue; but it is to avoid every kind and degree of sin, and to do the will of God with the whole heart.

This is what we undertook to perform—at our entrance into the Chriftian covenant. For then we folemnly renounced the world, the flefh and the devil; and promifed, that, in our future conduct and converfation, we fhould be fo far from fuffering ourfelves to be led by their fuggeftions, that, on the contrary,—we fhould be always attentive to the commandments of GOD, and walk in the fame all the days of our lives.

Then only are we "*Righteous*," when we fulfil the conditions of this obligation—when we live as becometh the Gofpel of CHRIST—when we avoid the corruption that is in the world—and cleanfe ourfelves from all filthinefs of flefh and fpirit, perfecting holinefs in the fear of GOD. And can that man, who purfues the popular modes and cuftoms of the world—who is anxioufly engaged in bufinefs, bafely immerfed mersed in pleasures, or uselessly sunk in indolence—ever imagine that he is acting the part of a true Christian, or likely to answer his baptismal engagements? Or can he, who, perceiving the vanity of these pursuits, has turned his thoughts to the concerns of his Soul, and made some progress in the way of Godliness, ever want to be convinced of the burden of his duty, and the difficulty of performing it as it ought to be done? Will not the trouble he finds in conquering his reluctancy to that which is good, and the constant diligence he is obliged to exert in curbing his propensity to that which is evil, sufficiently teach him the hardships of his undertaking? Does not the conflict he feels in subduing his passions, and restraining his appetites within proper bounds, plainly prove to him, that the practice of Religion is a difficult task? And yet, these are only the difficulties of his privacy—of that condition in which he is moſt ſecure. For—when he comes into the world, is aſſaulted by temptations on every ſide, and ſeduced by every ſenſe, what care and caution is he obliged to uſe, what vigour and reſolution is he forced to exert, what mortification and ſelf-denial is he bound to exerciſe, in order to withſtand their fatal influence, and maintain his integrity in ſuch dangerous attacks? Nay, and when he has done his utmoſt to keep his heart pure and undefiled, ſomething wrong, of one kind or other, will be continually ſliding in—to ſully his virtue, and to diſturb his peace.

But ſuppoſe that he has vanquiſhed all theſe difficulties:—that he has brought his paſſions under due regulation—hardened himſelf againſt the allurements of temptations—and conſequently can refrain from the

## SERMON XI.

the commiffion of evil; yet ftill he muft pafs through a painful ftage of active duties before he can attain the perfection of a Chriftian. For we are not only bound to efchew evil, but alfo commanded to do good: we are not only to refrain from vicious actions, but muft labour to advance in virtue, by the exercife of thofe duties, which we owe both to GOD and man.

To this end, we muft be conftant and devout in the worfhip of our GOD, and ready in all acts of benevolence to our neighbour. In the church we muft adore, in our clofets we muft meditate on, our Creator; we muft ferve him in all the ordinances he has prefcribed, and efpecially in the celebration of the LORD's fupper. And in all thefe applications to GOD, let us ever bear in mind, that our hearts muft be prepared and fanctified, and our affections kept warm and steady, left we should otherwise—not only offer an unprofitable sacrifice—but unhappily convert the means of our improvement into an occasion of sin, and instruments of destruction.

When we have thus discharged our duty to God, then our neighbour claims our attention. And with regard to *him*, how wide is the extent and compass of our duty? And how hard is it to accomplish those various demands, which daily and hourly spring upon us from some or other of the relations of life? And yet, any of these demands, left unaccomplished, render us defective in our Christian character, and criminal in the sight of God.

Now, if we reflect on these manifold obligations, and consider with ourselves, how much it is—that we owe to the honour and

and service of God, to the welfare and benefit of our neighbour, and to the instruction and discipline of our own Souls, we shall be so far from disputing the Apostle's assertion " of the Righteous being scarcely saved," that we shall rather be tempted, on such a view of Religion, to doubt the possibility of Salvation.

And indeed, were God so rigid a judge as to insist on a sinless and perfect observance of all these duties—were he extreme to remark whatever happened to be done amiss, without making any allowance for our infirmities,—what mortal could stand before him? But, to our comfort, there is mercy with him; and our labour is not in vain. For the sake of Christ, he is graciously pleased to overlook our failings; and to accept of sincerity instead of perfection. But then it must be remembered, and carefully remembered, that this sincerity plainly implies, that we vigorously exert all our endeavours; and study to obey him to the utmost of our power. Single acts of transgression, committed through surprise or weakness, are not of such malignity, as to cut us off from the love of God, or exclude us from the number of the Righteous. They are incident to our nature, and therefore pardonable. But wilful transgressions are of another kind; and he who so offends in any one point, is in effect guilty of the whole law. Pardon extends only to our imperfections—and not to our perverse, unrepented transgressions. If we cannot live up to an exact conformity with the precepts delivered, it is however incumbent upon us to come as near them as we possibly can. This is essential to Gospel-Righteousness: and our weakness is so far from rendering the burden of our duty lighter to us, that

it

it manifestly adds to the weight of it; and is itself an argument, that the Righteous can scarcely be saved.

But if this be the case of the virtuous and good, then, how sad must be the condition, and how terrible the prospect, of the ungodly and the sinner! If he, who is attentive to the calls of Religion, and industrious in his obedience to the commands of God—who strenuously labours to subdue his corruption, and to keep himself free from the pollutions of sin—if *this* man, I say, after all his trouble, does but scarcely attain to eternal happiness; then, what can *he*, who forgets God, and disregards his Religion—who profanes his Sabbaths, and neglects his worship—who gives himself up to the conduct of his passions, and riots in the practice of known sins; what can HE possibly expect,—but that

that he shall be forced to "eat of the bitter fruits of his own ways, and be filled at last with the wretched produce of his own devices?" Without Repentance and a Change of Life, his condition must be dreadful indeed. And if by the Grace of God he attempts to form in himself this Change, how hard a matter will he find it to keep close to the practice of Virtue, when he has been long accustomed to do evil? How often will his bad habits, even in spite of his care to suppress them, recover their strength, and lead him astray? And how slowly must the Graces of the Gospel, even under the strictest culture, thrive in so wayward an heart? What remorse must he feel for his offences past? And how anxious must he be for the time to come, lest the day of vengeance should unhappily overtake him, before he is delivered from the snares of sin, and has worked

worked himfelf into the favour of God? So difficult is it, even for the moft awakened finner, to perform thofe duties, and regain that ftate, upon which depends the promife of falvation. And yet, if thofe duties be not performed, and that virtuous ftate abfolutely recovered, he is loft and undone for ever. If he prefumptuoufly relies on the mercy of God, it is fit he fhould know, that this mercy is fufficiently fhewn in accepting his Repentance, and allowing him time to repent in. But if he does not, in the mean while, "bring forth fruits meet for repentance," and thoroughly amend his ways, there remains nothing for him but fearful denunciations of judgment and fiery indignation from the juftice of God.

"Let the wicked therefore forfake his ways, and the unrighteous man his thoughts;
and

and let him return unto the LORD, that he may have mercy upon him; and to his GOD, that he may pardon him." Let him feriously confider, that Religion is no trifling concern—no incidental bufinefs to be defpatched at pleafure; but a fervice of infinite importance—neceffary to be well and accurately performed, and yet very difficult to be fo accomplifhed. This confideration, if he has any love or regard for his foul, will inevitably roufe his care, and impel him forwards in the path of duty. But—is it only HIS care and attention—is it only the vigilance of the thoughtlefs finner—that wants thus to be raifed and improved? Have we not *all* of us, alas! great reafon to bewail our negligence in this refpect? How few are there among us, who think of Religion with the ferioufnefs they ought? And how very few, who practife the duties of it with the exact-
nefs

nefs they might? We acknowledge that we have faults that want to be corrected, and yet suffer them to remain: we acknowledge that there are virtues which it behoves us to acquire, and yet have not the spirit to labour for the attainment of them. But is this to act as we have the Righteous for an example, or as persons who mean to secure themselves? Consider, though you are now content—perhaps fully satisfied—with your present degree or measure of goodness, yet the time is hastening on, when you will see the necessity of higher attainments. When the Lord cometh with ten thousand of his Saints to render to every man according to his works, what ardent wishes shall we pour forth, that we had been more industrious in well-doing, and had fairer accounts to give? Let us therefore, I beseech you, be true and faithful to these dictates of nature; and so live

at

at prefent, as we fhall then be fure to wifh we had lived. The difficulties of falvation ought neither to difcourage the good, nor to deter the bad. Their ufe is to confirm the diligent, and to awaken the negligent— to increafe the refolution of the one, and to expel the indolence of the other. Happy BOTH, if they profit by them. If the one is encouraged to continue his courfe fo well begun ; and the other is perfuaded to reform his life, and provide for his happinefs by a fpeedy repentance.

# SERMON XII.

# SERMON XII.

### LUKE ii.—32.

A LIGHT TO LIGHTEN THE GENTILES.

To perſons who read the revealed account of the diſpenſations of providence towards mankind; that is, to perſons who read the Holy Scriptures, in a curſory and ſuperficial manner; it may ſeem perhaps,—as if God, though equally the Father of all, had not dealt with all—after the ſame equitable and impartial method.—It may ſeem perhaps, as if He were, in an high degree, a refpecter of perfons; remarkably attentive, and peculiarly favourable to fome of his children, and as remarkably regardlefs, and ftrangely neglectful of others.

Of this partiality fome think they difcover an undeniable inftance, in that diftinction He made between Jews and Gentiles. And indeed it cannot be denied, but that He did make, through a long feries of years, a very great and remarkable difference between them.

He feparated the Jews in early times, from all other nations, and took them under his own immediate guidance and protection. He honoured them with his prefence—fupported them by his miracles—favoured them with his covenant—directed them by his laws—awed them by his threats—and encouraged them by his promifes.

mifes. He was in a peculiar manner their God; and declared them to be his elect and chofen people—his fpecial and peculiar inheritance.

In the mean while, the reft of mankind, comprehended under the common name of Gentiles, remained in appearance deftitute and forlorn—aliens from the commonwealth of Ifrael—ftrangers to the covenant of promife—without God, without revelation, without knowledge, and without hope, in the world.

The difference of their condition is therefore manifeft; and the conduct which produced it may appear, in a contracted view, unworthy of that wife and gracious Being, whofe care as well as mercy is over all his works. But if we extend our profpect around, and take in the comprehenfive circuit

cuit of his proceedings, we shall see reason to correct our first conclusion, and to adore the wisdom and goodness of his providence; which, through this seemingly unequal administration, has been constantly and uniformly operating to one great and glorious end—the real happiness of the whole world.

For God dispensed the light of Revelation, and declared his will to the sons of men, in such a manner as was most expedient on so extraordinary an occasion—in such a degree as was best adapted to their several apprehensions—and at a time when it was most likely to produce its proper effects.

When ignorance and superstition prevailed in the world, and men were lost in the errors of idolatry, God was pleased to call

call forth Abraham, the great founder of the Jewish nation, and to make him large and precious promises. He called *him* forth, because he was a man of singular piety—a fit person to *propagate* that true Religion to which he had so firmly and steadily adhered: God made him those promises to strengthen his faith, and to encourage his endeavours in that great work, which he had appointed him to execute. For, as he had declared, that the Messiah, in whom all the nations of the earth were to be blessed, was to spring from his loins; so he appointed *him* and his posterity to reform and improve the rest of the world; and to convey down the glad tidings of that signal mercy that was finally intended for them.

Accordingly, when he had thus made these pious Patriarchs public vouchers of his

his Being and Providence, and teachers of his true Religion; he fent them out to bear his name before the nations; and to inftruct them in the ways of truth and righteoufnefs. Out they proceeded, and God went with them; difplayed himfelf miraculoufly before them—not for their fakes alone, but alfo, to make his power known among the Heathen, and his Divinity acknowledged to the ends of the earth.

With the fame gracious view to the general improvement of mankind, when he brought up the Ifraelites from the land of Egypt, he placed them in the centre of the moft diftinguifhed nations; and put them under fuch a difpenfation, as muft prove in the event equally beneficial to the world, whether they obeyed him or obeyed him not. When they obeyed God, they profpered; and the nations flowed in unto them,

them, and were enlightened. When they difobeyed him, they were punifhed with captivity; and, fcattered among the nations, taught them ftill. So that in either cafe, the Gentiles were fure to gain knowledge and inftruction of them.

How marvellous are the counfels of God! and how wife his proceedings! But we have not yet confidered all.

For when he had, by the difcipline of the Mofaic œconomy, recovered the Jews from their defection and idolatry, and brought them to the obedience and acknowledgment of Himfelf; he left them, as it were, for a time, and turned his regard, after a more efpecial manner, to the Gentiles. In confequence of this regard, He raifed up among them a fucceffion of philofophers, who may juftly be looked

upon

upon as so many heathen apostles; labouring for the improvement of that part of the world, in a way adapted to the genius and circumstances of the people they taught.

These men clearly saw the depraved state of human nature; and therefore strongly inculcated the great necessity of Reformation. They plainly perceived the gross absurdities of the reigning superstitions; and therefore warmly inveighed against them. They considerably cleared up the nature and attributes of the Deity; and re-established on a tolerable foundation the chief principles of natural religion. Truths, indeed many—and important truths—there were, which they could in no wise discover. What they did discover had however its effects; and greatly forwarded the purposes of Providence. If

they

they could not entirely difpel the darknefs, they thinned it to admiration. They corrected errors, removed obftructions, and opened the way to fublimer doctrines, fhould any fuch be offered.

And fuch, by the kindly defignation of Providence, did offer foon. For, about this time, the Hebrew Scriptures were tranflated into Greek; and by that means conveyed down ftill greater knowledge to the Gentiles. In thefe Scriptures they faw the tenets of their philofophers, in feveral points, confirmed; fettled on a furer bafis, and raifed to higher perfection. From thefe Scriptures they learned befides, many things of which before they had no intimations. They learned in particular, that a Perfon was fhortly to come, who fhould make up the defects of reafon and philofophy; declare to the world the whole will

will of God; and supply it with the means of life and happiness. Hence, they were prompted ardently to wish for the arrival of this Person. In that wish the scheme of Providence had its effect: for it was the principal aim of all his difpensations, to render men sensible of the neceffity of a Redeemer, and desirous at last of his coming.

In the fulness of time, when Jews and Gentiles were in expectation of him, Christ appeared in the world. And, though He came as the great Teacher of all mankind, yet His first concern as God's before, was to instruct and reform the children of Ifrael. The Jews had still the preference. But their prerogative was soon abolished; and the divine favours, like divine providence, were extended to all people.

For,

# SERMON XII.

For, when our Saviour had explained the more obscure doctrines of their law, and placed the sanctions of it in a clearer light—when He had corrected their mistakes concerning its precepts, and refined them to greater sublimity—in short, when He had given the Jews a perfect system of faith and morals, confirmed by miracles, and exemplified in practice; He put an end to all distinctions, and, as Lord of all, commissioned the apostles to apply to all, and make disciples of every nation.

In the power of this commission they went forth, and published the Gospel to every creature—the Lord working with them, and bearing testimony to the doctrines they taught by the signs and wonders He enabled them to perform.

Now,

Now, the Gentiles were enlightened indeed. For where reason could arrive at no degree of knowledge respecting some important, saving truths; there the Gospel has been a light to them in the most proper sense; by revealing what they were utterly ignorant of, though, at the same time, was necessary to be known.

Where they entertained before some faint and doubtful notions of things; there they were advanced by the preaching of the apostles to assurance and certainty.

Where they acknowledged reverence and obedience to be due to God; there they were taught to worship him after a Spiritual manner, and to serve him with a pure heart.

Where

## SERMON XII.    255

Where they wanted directions in the various ſtates and relations of life; there they were furniſhed with proper rules, plain to be underſtood, and eaſy to be applied when occaſion required. In a word, Christ hath abounded towards them in all wiſdom and in all knowledge; made them complete in Himſelf; and endowed them, according to his divine power, with every thing neceſſary to life and happineſs.

It is true, there are ſeveral myſteries, relating to the nature and eſſence of God—ſeveral myſteries, relating to his kingdom, which are not made known unto men: nor is it requiſite they ſhould be. For the light which our Saviour brought, the knowledge which the Goſpel communicates, is quite ſufficient to the purpoſes of ſalvation—ſufficient to guide us in the ways of holineſs through the courſe of this life,

and

and to bring us to happiness in the life to come. This is all we really want. And since our wants are in this respect so well supplied, it would be folly to complain that our curiosity is not gratified.

When therefore the Day-spring from on high was pleased to visit us; He shed sufficient light around to lighten every man that cometh into the world—a light that shines with this peculiar advantage; that it is clear and perceptible to all.

It required both a close application and deep reach of thought—qualities not very common—to find out the sentiments and opinions of the philosophers: and the typical, hidden meaning of the Jewish law was perhaps still more difficult to be discovered. But the Gospel delivers the most exalted truths in a plain familiar style,

adap-

adapted to the meanest capacities. The sense in most places—in all places of importance—is obvious at first sight; so that every one who readeth the Gospel may easily understand it. And we of the Reformed Churches may read it in our language; and consequently must thank our own negligence, if we know not as much as we are concerned to know, in order to be happy.

For it is further to be observed, that our gracious LORD, to render this light more effectual, has been pleased to shed forth the Spirit of Truth into our hearts, whose office it is to lead us into all needful truths; and to impress them on our minds and consciences. If we study therefore the scripture with care, and seek knowledge in the love thereof; we may rest assured, that we shall know so much of the doctrine, as is necessary to instruct us in the nature of

S our

our duty, and to encourage us in the practice of it.

We have now feen the whole progrefs of God's adminiftration, as it relates to the improvement of mankind. From the view we have taken, it plainly appears that he bore throughout an equal regard to all his children. It plainly appears, that he was in reality the God of the Gentiles, as well as of the Jews, though he treated them in a different manner. His defign was to inftruct and reform them both; and he wifely applied himfelf to each, according as they were capable of being benefited by him. If fome remained in darknefs longer than others, it was, becaufe they were unable to bear the light: and if fome are fuffered ftill to continue in the fame fituation, it is, probably, owing to the fame reafon.

The prophecy however is fulfilled: and *we* of this nation are happy witnesses of its accomplishment. For *we* were once Gentiles, as deeply involved in darkness and obscurity as any of our benighted brethren: but out of this darkness God in his mercy called us forth into a marvellous light—a light that shines upon *us* with the purest rays and the strongest lustre; and which therefore it behoves us carefully to apply to the use it was intended to serve.

Now the use of this light is to direct our steps, and guide our feet into the way of peace. Let us then be guided by it. Let us walk honestly as in the day—not in vice and vanity, as those who know not God; but in righteousness and holiness, conformably with our profession.

## SERMON XII.

The Gospel requires a conversation suitable to its doctrines; and justly expects that we should improve in virtue, as the means of it improve upon us. But the means of Salvation which *we* enjoy are indeed exceedingly great; and great should be our proficiency under them: else these advantages, instead of contributing to our comfort and happiness, will become articles of accusation against us, and increase both our guilt and punishment.

Besides, if we persist in the abuse of this signal mercy, if we neglect the light so graciously afforded, GOD may judicially withdraw it from us, as He did from others, in the like case, before us. Nay, though He should not withdraw it by any particular act of his avenging providence, our own inattention, negligence and vices would by degrees, in the natural course of things, totally

totally fupprefs and extinguifh it. For how can Religion fubfift where it is not profeffed? And how can it be faid to be profeffed, where its fervices are not attended? The contempt therefore of public worfhip, fo flagrant among us, is one of the greateft inftances of unthankfulnefs to God, and of injury to his Gofpel, of which we can be guilty. It is in effect to put out the light which God has kindled; and to endeavour to bring the world back to that wretched ftate of ignorance and error, in which it lay before it was illuminated.

This confideration will, I hope, prevail upon thofe, who are not quite loft to virtue and goodnefs, to make it a real point of confcience, not to abfent themfelves unneceffarily from the ordinances of God, or the places of public worfhip. For there the word is read and explained; the facraments

are

## SERMON XII.

are duly administered; and many peculiar helps to Salvation offered. And if we faithfully use these helps—recollect, impress and apply what we hear—we shall no longer be either inactive or unfruitful in the knowledge of our LORD JESUS CHRIST; but shall be moved thereby to the constant practice of those virtues and graces, which serve to render us acceptable to GOD, and approved of men.

Now we know these things, happy are we if we do them. And do them we should, for the sake of Religion as well as of ourselves. Holiness of life is not only the end, but also the support, of Religion. It is to this that Christianity owes, in a great measure, its growth and propagation. Had it not been for the virtues of its first professors, we had never been partakers of the Gospel. Their practice recommended it to our forefathers; and ours should recommend it to our children. If

If then we have any concern for the honour of God, any concern for the advancement of virtue, any concern for the welfare of posterity, let us daily endeavour with the utmost assiduity to adorn the doctrine of our Saviour in all things. Fully sensible that our profession will always be estimated by our actions; let us be careful to shew by our good conversation the noble principles that are ingrafted in our Souls: let us make our light so to shine before men, that they may see our good works; and, allured by their excellency, may be induced to quit the ways of error, and perform the same to the glory of God.

# SERMON XIII.

# SERMON XIII.

ACTS iv.—27, 28.

FOR OF A TRUTH, AGAINST THY HOLY CHILD JESUS, WHOM THOU HAST ANOINTED, BOTH HEROD AND PONTIUS PILATE, WITH THE GENTILES AND THE PEOPLE OF ISRAEL, WERE GATHERED TOGETHER, FOR TO DO WHATEVER THY HAND AND THY COUNSEL DETERMINED BEFORE TO BE DONE.

As there was a general and ſtrong expectation of the Meſſiah's coming, both among Jews and Gentiles, at the time our Saviour

Saviour appeared in the world; it might naturally be prefumed, when he took upon him the character of that expected Prophet, that all would have been ready to attend to his claim, and allow his pretenfions an equitable hearing;—that, confidering the defign he came upon, and the proofs he gave of the truth of his miffion, all would have fincerely believed on his name, and yielded a willing obedience to his authority.

But neverthelefs, hiftory fhews, that the reception he met with, was, in fact, extremely different. For both the Jews and Gentiles, inftead of examining the merits of his caufe, malicioufly joined in a confederacy againft him; and profecuted their refentment even to death.—Now, fuch a conduct is a clear indication of an extraordinary, and violent prejudice. Yet, as he he appeared exactly at the time when he was expected, you may wonder how they could possibly be prejudiced against him. But the *time* of his appearance was not the thing: the offence was taken at the manner of it; which was juft the reverfe of what they had imagined.

The *Jews* were deeply poffeffed with the notion, that the Meffiah would appear in all the fplendor and majefty of power; and reftore the kingdom to Ifrael. Such was the redemption they had formerly experienced, and fuch was the redemption they now expected.

The *Gentiles* entertained a different opinion: for they thought, that he would come in the fpirit of the ancient philofophers; and reform the world by the united force of eloquence and learning.

In

In confequene of thefe notions, the Jews required a fign—and the Greeks fought after wifdom: but, the former could fee no fign of conqueft, no fymbols of royalty, in the humble deportment and mean condition of JESUS CHRIST; nor could the others find the fubtleties and refinement of philofophy in his plain and fimple doctrine. Hence both of them immediately concluded, that fuch a perfon, deftitute, as they thought, of the neceffary qualifications, could never be the intended author of falvation. For a *crucified* Saviour was to the *Jews* a *ftumbling-block*, and to the *Greeks foolifhnefs*.

So great was the offence of the crofs, in the firft ages of the Gofpel. It continued to prevail in later times: nor is it yet, perhaps, quite removed. For fome may ftill imagine, that, if JESUS had been truly the

## SERMON XIII.

Son of GOD, and the glorious Redeemer of mankind, divine wifdom would have hardly directed, that he fhould appear in fo mean and obfcure a condition ; much lefs would divine juftice have ever permitted, that he fhould experience fuch great and terrible fufferings.

Now, to clear up this point, and, if I can, to remove the fcruples you may entertain concerning it ; I fhall prove in the firft place, that JESUS CHRIST was truly the promifed Redeemer; the holy child of GOD, whom he had anointed for the falvation of the world. And then I fhall fhew in the fecond place, that, as in the circumftances of his life, and the manner of his death, there was nothing—but what GOD had before determined ; fo there was nothing—but what is perfectly reconcileable to his wifdom and goodnefs. In the
firft

first place then, I am to prove, that JESUS CHRIST was truly the promised Redeemer, the Holy Child of GOD, whom he had anointed for the salvation of the world. Now, if we argue with the Jews on their own principles, bringing the cause of CHRIST to the test of the Mosaic law, and trying his claim by the prophecies of ancient Scripture, it has been already proved, and the proof is on record, that He is the true Messiah. St. Stephen proved it in this way long ago to the council at Jerusalem; and so did St. Paul to the Jews at Antioch. Their proof, it is true, is very short; and deduced only from the completion of some few prophecies; but collect all the predictions from Moses to Malachi, that have any relation to the expected Redeemer, and you will find them every one fulfilled in JESUS CHRIST—fulfilled in so plain and perfect a manner; that, from being formerly

merly to the Jews the great fupport of their faith, they are now become to them a ftanding reproof for their infidelity. And the ftronger reproof, as the caufe of their prejudice is taken away. For how defpicable foever this fame Jesus might appear to them in the days of his humiliation and weaknefs; yet, one would think, they might, even on their own views, have fince been fully reconciled to him, by the glory of his kingdom, and the mightinefs of his power.

But perhaps this manifeft conformity between the character of Christ and the ancient prophefies is not the proof upon which you would reft. You rather choofe, with the Gentile, to examine his pretenfions by the rule of reafon; and determine their validity by the correfpondence they bear to the dictates of wifdom. Let us fee then,

then, whether the truth of his miffion may not be fupported upon this footing, and juftified by the propriety of it. It is the judgment of the author of the epiftle to the Hebrews, that " fuch an high Prieft" or Saviour " became us," that is, was needful for us, " who is holy, harmlefs, un-" defiled, feparate from finners, and made " higher than the heavens." Now, let Reafon fpeak, and it will form exactly the fame judgment. For, as we had ftrayed into the paths of wickednefs and mifery, and were ignorant of the means of attaining to happinefs; did we not evidently ftand in need of the affiftance of fome wife and holy perfon, who could inftruct us in all neceffary truths by his doctrine, and would guide us by his example into the ways of Righteoufnefs? And moreover; as the juftice of God, required fatisfaction for the offence our fins had given to his

holi-

## SERMON XIII.

holinefs; and as this fatisfaction could not be made—but either by our own deaths, or, after all the indulgences of mercy, by the death of a pure unfpotted fubftitute of the fame kind; then, did we not likewife ftand in need of the friendly interpofal of fome innocent, meritorious perfon, could fuch be found, who would be willing to fuffer and to die for us? But neverthelefs, though our tranfgreffions were forgiven, and ourfelves delivered from mifery; yet alas! confidering the depravity of our difpofitions, and the imperfection of our beft fervices, both owing to our own fault, we might ftill juftly defpair, without the interceffion of a powerful advocate, of gaining accefs to the pure majefty of Heaven, in whofe prefence alone is the fulnefs of joy and happinefs.

Now, if the wants and neceffities of human nature were fuch; and fuch the measures of relief, which human reason would judge expedient; surely Reason may be well content: for CHRIST is, according to this very form, the wisdom of GOD unto Salvation.

Did we want to be instructed in the knowledge of our duty, and to be excited to the practice of it? Then behold! CHRIST has not only given us a perfect and complete rule of life for the direction of our conduct in every situation; but has likewise enforced and recommended it to us by a continued course of well-doing; "leaving us an example, that we should follow his steps." And though the doctrines he taught, and the precepts he delivered, carried in them plain evidence of their divine original; yet to remove all doubt, that they were not his own, but the Father's who sent him, he performed such works in in confirmation of them, as no man could perform, except God were with him.

Again; did we stand in need of a meritorious sacrifice to make atonement for our past transgressions? Then behold! Jesus Christ, when he had fulfilled all righteousness, voluntarily endured the punishment due to our iniquities, and offered himself a sacrifice to God for our ransom. And as he died for our sins, so he rose again for our justification: and is now ascended to the right hand of the Majesty on high, where he ever liveth to make intercession for us.

These things Jesus did. And, in the eye of Reason, does he not appear from what he has done, to have fully answered the character of the Redeemer? " So far, " perhaps you will admit, he has: but yet, " there

"there were several circumstances attending his life, that seem to be scarce consistent with that character. For, if he had been truly the Saviour of the world, can it ever be supposed, he would have been sent into the world in so mean and abject a manner; much less, that he would have been brought at last to suffer such a cruel and ignominious death?"

Now, these things, however they may appear at first sight, are, in reality, so far from being any objections to the truth of Christ's mission, that, as I am going to shew in the

Second place, they rather tend to confirm and establish it. For, should not Christ, when he came into the world, have been placed in those circumstances which contributed most to the accomplishment

ment of his defign? Now, his defign, you know, was to fave the world: and one way of effecting this, was by preaching and inftructing men in the knowledge of their duty. But, how could he inftruct them, unlefs he converfed familiarly with them? And what ftate of life could afford him fuch great opportunities of converfing familiarly with them, and fpreading the Gofpel among them, as the low, wandering condition in which he appeared? It was right, you may grant, he fhould travel about: but it fhould have been in pomp and fplendor; for that would have fecured refpect to his perfon, and have alfo added authority to his doctrine. But how wrong, alas! do we judge of things! Suppofe CHRIST had come, as the Jews expected, in the form of a mighty prince, and had propagated his religion in all the magnificence of earthly power, what would have

have been the confequence? Would not *that* nation have heard it with awe and wonder? would they not have taken it upon truft, without examination? and have eagerly embraced it, not for its excellency, but for their own intereft? And might not *other* nations be induced to reject it on this very account? deeming it the work of human policy, calculated on purpofe to bring *them* to flavery and fubjection.

Whereas, by appearing in the manner he did, he fhewed to the world, that he had himfelf no temporal views; and that others could have no motive to become his difciples, but their firm belief in the truth of his doctrines.

But there was another thing which Christ was to perform for the falvation of the

the world—and that was, to exemplify our duty in his own conduct, and exhibit in his own person a pattern for us to copy. And in what situation could he perform this with the same advantage, as in that which he chose? Had he assumed the state and ensigns of royalty, and framed his life to that character, his example could have been but of little use to the general part of mankind. The virtues, which he then must have chiefly exercised, would have been of a high and lofty nature, instances of power, and acts of munificence—which yet, as it was, he more gloriously displayed by a series of merciful and gracious miracles. But by taking, as he did, that humble station, and encountering those hardships and temptations, which press most heavily on human life, he rendered himself such an example of virtue, as the necessities of mankind required. An example of humility, meek-nefs and patience; an example of contentednefs, refignation and forgivenefs—virtues' for which we have daily occafion, and which are yet fo difficult of attainment, that herein we wanted moft of all the guidance and encouragement of a precedent.

This then juftifies the manner of his appearance. But it is further objected—did not this perfon, who, we fay, is our Redeemer, fuffer at laft; and die the moft contemptible and ignominious death? We own he did. And does not this complete the evidence of his being the Meffiah? For ought not CHRIST to have fuffered? How elfe fhould the Scriptures be fulfilled, which long had foretold—that thus it muft be? How elfe would the redemption of the world have been perfectly accomplifhed? For the principal method by which he was to redeem us, was the making himfelf a fubftitute

tute for us; paying in his own body the penalty of our fins; and fo procuring us the remiffion of them. But the wages of fin is death; and God had determined, that without fhedding of blood there fhould be no remiffion. It was therefore neceffary, that Christ, who came to redeem us from death, fhould, to accomplifh that redemption, die himfelf in our ftead. And fince our releafe depends upon his death, the more ignominious and public it was, the more it tends to ftrengthen our fecurity. But ftill, you may fay, it is a great reproach. It would have been, had he continued the prifoner of the grave. But to our comfort, and to our honour too, the infamy of his death was foon fwallowed up by the glory of his refurrection.

But it is further urged—where was the neceffity of his dying at all; fince God could have

have freely pardoned us without any atonement? What GOD *could* do, it becomes not us to judge. What he *has* done, we know: and we may conclude, that for so doing he had good reasons. Had he vouchsafed to forgive us, without exacting any satisfaction, we must indeed have admired the abundance of his mercy; but then, we should not so fully have discovered, what it greatly concerns us to be apprised of, the infinite malignity of sin, and the infinite abhorrence GOD has to it—we should not so fully have discovered the zealous concern he entertains for the honour of his laws, nor the great necessity there is of our living conformably with them. Now, in the redemption purchased by the death of CHRIST, all these points are clearly displayed; at the same time that the mercy of GOD is equally manifested. In this view then, this method of Salvation, which the Greek

Phi-

## SERMON XIII. 285

Philofophers called foolifhnefs, is far fuperior in wifdom to any fcheme that man can devife. For let him devife what he will, it muft ever appear either too rigorous or too mild. But here is a difpenfation wifely attempered between the feverity of juftice and the lenity of mercy. A difpenfation, wherein the frailty of human nature is gracioufly confidered and provided for, and the honour of the divine majefty vindicated and maintained. A difpenfation, which affords the finner all the fecurity he can wifh, for his deliverance from the punifhment of his paft tranfgreffions; and lays before him all the motives he can want, for his future improvement in piety and virtue.

SERMON

# SERMON XIV.

# SERMON XIV.

**JOHN xiv.—16.**

I WILL PRAY THE FATHER, AND HE SHALL GIVE YOU ANOTHER COMFORTER, THAT HE MAY ABIDE WITH YOU FOR EVER.

WHEN the Disciples understood that their Master was shortly to leave the world, they looked upon themselves to be, as in the ordinary view of things they indeed were, in a very deplorable, distressed condition. They were engaged in a work, which

which their own obfervation could affure them was attended throughout with an infinite variety of the moft grievous hardfhips. They faw what their Mafter fuffered; and were taught to expect, whenever he was gone, that the fame would fall upon themfelves. The gloominefs of the profpect which they had before them naturally alarmed their fears; and the apprehenfion of the calamities coming upon them filled their hearts with forrow.

In this fituation of things, it would have agreed as ill with our SAVIOUR's tendernefs, as with the exigence of his Religion, to have fuffered the Difciples to remain comfortlefs. Their cafe required peculiar attention; and, as it was in itfelf uncommon, called aloud for uncommon relief. Such relief was gracioufly adminiftered to them— fufficient to allay the terror of their minds, and

and to reconcile them to the hardships o. their duty. For if the hardships of their duty were great, they had this assurance from their Master to comfort them, that great also would be the reward of their fidelity, in the place he was going to prepare for them.

If their nature was too weak and frail to withstand the shocks of so many dangers, they had still in him such a powerful advocate with the Father, that whatever succour or assistance they should ask in his name, should effectually be granted to them.

If they were anxious and concerned lest the cause they had undertaken, and which had hitherto prospered in virtue chiefly of their Master's presence, should fail in their hands when he was departed; they were seasonably relieved with this further promise, that as soon as he was gone, he would send one from heaven to supply his absence.—One that should espouse and defend their cause: conduct and manage what they had in charge: and render them by his influence superior, at last, to all opposition: one that should never leave, nor forsake them; but should continue with them, and with those who believed through them, to the end of the world. " I will pray the Father, and he shall " give you another comforter, that he " may abide with you for ever."

Now, the accomplishment of this promise, in the actual descent of the HOLY GHOST upon the Apostles, is what the Church commemorates—most deservedly commemorates—on this day; since, without such provision, it must necessarily have failed

## SERMON XIV.

failed and perished from the earth. For how strong soever the foundation had been laid by the hand of Omnipotence; yet nothing less than the seasonable communication of the same power could have enabled those, who were to build thereon, to advance, support and complete the work. After what manner this power was exerted in the days of the Apostles, and how far it continues to operate at present:—or, according to another form of words, in what instances the Holy Spirit formerly was, and still is, an advocate for the Christian cause, is what I shall now endeavour to explain.

When the HOLY SPIRIT came down from Heaven, the state of the Church, or, of the Christian cause was briefly this.

JESUS

## SERMON XIV.

Jesus Christ was sent into the world to inform mankind of the will of God; and to inftruct them in the way to eternal falvation. He came to thofe who were peculiarly his own, that is, to the Jews; but they were fo far from believing him to be that great Prophet, whom their Scripture taught them to expect, that they looked upon him as a daring impoftor; and inftead of receiving him with the efteem and veneration due to his character, they perfecuted, reviled, and murdered him. Before his death, indeed, he founded a Religion in every refpect worthy of God, as in every refpect beneficial to man. He confirmed this Religion by miracles; and exemplified it in his converfation. To unprejudiced minds this might be fufficient to prove its Divinity; but with thofe of another caft, the fufferings of its Author might ftand as an evidence of the falfity of his

his religion; and the ignominy of his death as a demonſtration of his impoſture.

In theſe circumſtances, common reaſon dictates to us, that ſomething was needful to be done, to ſupport our Saviour's claim, and to juſtify the truth of his miſſion:—that ſomething was needful to be done, to vindicate his perſonal innocence; and to illuſtrate the equity of God in permitting him to ſuffer ſuch cruel treatment:—that ſomething was needful to be done, to ſhew that God, though he thought proper to permit it, yet did not countenance that conſpiracy againſt him.

Theſe points the world might expect ſhould be cleared up: nor were they left to expect in vain: for theſe points the Spirit had in charge to vindicate. " When " he

## SERMON XIV.

" he is come, fays our Saviour, he will re-
" prove or convince the world, of fin,
" and of righteoufnefs, and of judgment.
" Of fin, becaufe they believe not on me:
" Of righteoufnefs, becaufe I go to my
" Father, and ye fee me no more: Of
" judgment, becaufe the prince of this
" world is judged." And accordingly,
when he came he convinced them effectually. For,

1. He gave them an undeniable proof of the truth of our Saviour's miffion by his very appearance in favour of his caufe. As the HOLY SPIRIT, and confe-quently the gifts of prophecy and mira-cles, had been withdrawn from the Jewifh Church above four hundred years, his vifible defcent on the Apoftles of CHRIST, after fo long an intermiffion, and accord-ing to the exprefs promife of their Mafter,
muft

must be to the Jews as clear an evidence as they could possibly desire of his being the prophet come from GOD. And if the scandal of his cross had so blinded their eyes that they could not see their sin in rejecting him; this event, this manifestation of his glory was sufficient in reason to correct their prejudices, and to bring them over to repentance. After this their infidelity became inexcusable. Especially, when we consider,

2. That the great power and dignity with which CHRIST was invested in heaven —evinced likewise by this effusion of the HOLY SPIRIT—was a manifest indication of his innocence. For it is agreed on all hands, that the righteous only can appear in the presence, or will be accepted in the sight, of GOD.

And

And though he seemed to be chaftifed in this world as a criminal, yet, in reality, it was the chaftifement of our fins that was upon him. He fuffered for us; the juft for the unjuft, that he might bring us to GOD. Wherefore GOD alfo exalted him to his own right-hand; and, for the fuffering of death made him both Lord and Chrift; " having given him a name which is above every name—fo that at the name of JESUS every knee fhall bow." And to convince them moreover that, though he permitted, he did not approve of their mercilefs proceedings, GOD difplayed the rigour of his judgment on the authors of our SAVIOUR's fufferings; as well on the Jews, who were the immediate inftruments; as on the prince of this world, by whofe inftigation they were excited to inflict them. For the Jews were overthrown by an almoft total deftruction · and as the Gofpel prevailed,

the

the power of Satan gradually decreafed:—the oracles were ftruck dumb—the Gods of the heathen were put to flight—their temples were demolifhed—their idols broken down—their facrifices difufed—and their worfhip detefted. In fhort, the head of the ferpent was mortally bruifed, and the power of darknefs was vanquifhed:—the Religion of CHRIST was vindicated in the world, and his kingdom effectually eftablifhed.

The divine miffion of our SAVIOUR, and the truth of his Religion being thus confirmed, we are next to confider what was further neceffary in order to fupport and propagate it.

Now, as this Religion was intended for the benefit of all nations, it was requifite that all nations fhould poffefs the means of

know-

knowing it. But this could never be done, in any reafonable time, nor perhaps with any confiderable efficacy, but by conferring on the Teachers of it the gift of Languages, to qualify them to inftruct and convert the Gentiles. And therefore when the Holy Ghoft fell on the Apoftles, he uſhered his adminiftration with this very gift. For " they all fpake with tongues, " as the Spirit gave them utterance."

When they were thus qualified to inftruct the world, the next thing requifite was, that the Doctrines in which they were to inftruct them ſhould be fo treafured in their minds, that none of them might be forgotten and loft. But this was more than their natural abilities could enfure. And therefore it was another part of the Spirit's office to bring all things to their remembrance,

brance, whatsoever their Master had said unto them.

But then, as it was not sufficient only to remember the doctrine of our SAVIOUR, but necessary likewise rightly to understand it; so the Holy Spirit secured them from error, by guiding them into all truth, and illuminating their understandings to judge unerringly of matters of faith.

Furnished however as they were for the work, yet there was still required an uncommon zeal to undertake it—an undaunted courage to pursue it—and an unparalleled patience to bear up against the constant hardships which every where attended it. But in all these things they were more than conquerors. For the Holy Ghost inspired them with such a degree of courage and firmness, that they feared no
oppo-

oppofition, declined no difficulties, dreaded no dangers in difcharge of their duty, but even rejoiced that they were thought worthy to fuffer for the name of CHRIST.

But, notwithftanding the conftancy, courage and affiduity of its firft teachers, a doctrine, fo contrary to the prevailing difpofitions of mankind, could make but a flow progrefs in a fenfual world by its own force. Men immerfed in the pleafures of fenfe are with difficulty brought to attend to reafon. Such can only be inftructed by being firft aftonifhed; and are fcarcely led to obey till they fee it is in vain to withftand.

Wherefore, in the laft place, the Holy Ghoft, as was neceffary, armed the Apoftles and firft converts to Chriftianity with the power of working miracles; which, at the fame time that they confirmed the truth of

## SERMON XIV.

of their doctrines, awakened the attention, and subdued the stubbornness of their hearers.

These are the principal instances wherein the Church, in its infant state, both required and received the assistance of the Spirit. And what was the result—what was the consequence of these wonderful manifestations? Why this.—A Religion that had nothing of external charms—that was quite contrary to the worldly interests and carnal inclinations of mankind—a Religion whose chief article was to believe in a despised and crucified Saviour—a Religion that proposed nothing to its professors, on earth, but tribulation, affliction, persecution and death—a Religion preached only by a set of poor, illiterate, contemptible mechanicks, and at the same time opposed—virulently opposed by the

rich

rich, the learned, and the honourable of the world—this Religion, under the influence of the SPIRIT, its advocate, broke through all reftraints and impediments—fpread itfelf with furprifing rapidity—fubdued all earthly powers—till kings after kings became obedient to it, and nations after nations did, and do it fervice.

How long thefe extraordinary powers continued in the Church, is a queftion that cannot eafily, and needs not critically, be determined. Thus much however the nature of the thing itfelf will fuggeft—that as they were conferred in order to evince the truth of the Gofpel, and to promote its reception in the world; fo they were continued as long as it required or ftood in want of fuch credentials. As the prejudices of mankind began to abate, thefe extraordinary manifeftations, which were
de-

designed to conquer them, we may suppose abated likewise; and at length totally ceased when Christianity was thoroughly established.

But nevertheless, though the HOLY SPIRIT does not, because he needs not, display himself at this time in such stupendous operations, yet he is still present with his Church, and will abide with it unto the end of the world.

After what manner he now abides with it, and in what measure he is an Advocate for it, we cannot pretend to say. But of this we are certain, and in this certainty we should rest content; that—as he operated formerly in the high degree that was necessary to establish it, so he operates still in that degree, whatever it be, which is necessary to preserve it. In consequence

of

of his care for the prefervation of the Church, he has conftituted an order of men to watch over its concerns—to maintain its worfhip—to preach its doctrines—and to adminifter its facraments. In thefe offices he is ever prefent with them, invigorating the outward means to the improvement of inward piety. He is likewife prefent with all its members, forwarding their endeavours in the way of falvation. To this end, he opens our underftandings to fee our duty, and influences our wills to put it in practice—he inftils into our minds good defires, and fuggefts to our reafon the moft powerful motives. He gives us ftrength to refift temptations, and grace to purify our affections—he fupports us with comfort in well-doing here, and affures us of happinefs for fo doing hereafter.

This

## SERMON XIV.

This he now does: and this is now sufficient. If any thing be wanting, it is our own concurrence. For though sanctification is the proper and genuine work of the Spirit, yet it is requisite, that we should comply with his motions to make them effectual.

Let it therefore be our great care to attend with seriousness to his suggestions, and to yield ourselves with humility to his guidance. When any good thoughts spring up in our minds—any good resolutions are formed in our hearts, let us cherish them by devotion, improve them by reflection, and at every opportunity bring them forth into life and action. If we are thus careful to improve these common graces of the Spirit which are now vouchsafed us, how far soever they may fall short of those which the Disciples formerly enjoyed,

enjoyed, yet we shall find them fully adequate to all the neceffities of our prefent condition—fufficient to carry us through the difficulties of our duty, and to bring us at laft to eternal glory. Let us then thankfully acknowledge our dependance on God for thefe ineftimable bleffings; and apply to him with fervour for the continuance of them; that fo, by the infpiration of the Holy Spirit, we may always think thofe things that be good, and by his merciful guiding may perform the fame, through Jesus Christ our Lord.

SERMON

# SERMON XV.

# SERMON XV.

### JOHN xxi.—22.

JESUS SAITH UNTO HIM, " IF I WILL THAT
" HE TARRY TILL I COME, WHAT IS THAT
" TO THEE? FOLLOW THOU ME."

AT the fifteenth verſe of this Chapter we find our Saviour queſtioning St. Peter concerning the truth and ſincerity of that love and regard which he profeſſed to have for his Lord and mafter;—whether he was now determined, after thofe repeated denials of him, to exhibit to the world a proof of his integrity by a ftedfaft adherence to him and to his caufe. When Peter anfwered that he was, if he knew his heart; and declared it thrice in confirmation of his fincerity; our Saviour told him, that, in confequence thereof, he muft diligently attend to the office of his ftation; and affiduoufly feed the flock of CHRIST, with the care of which he was now intrufted. The great motives to the vigorous performance of this duty, the great reward which he and the other Apoftles would obtain, if they continued faithful, CHRIST had elfewhere laid before them; all that he does here is to fupport the diffidence of St. Peter, and to encourage him to go on in the affurance of his fincerity: for he could now certify him, that his heart

was

was right and fixed; that, notwithstanding his faith had once failed him, he should henceforth persevere firm and constant to the end; that he would boldly encounter every hardship in the way of his ministry; and at last lay down his life for the glory of God, and the truth of the Gospel. Such was his duty; and such was to be his fate.

Now, St. Peter having heard his own fate determined, and seeing the Disciple whom Jesus loved, his curiosity prompted him to ask his Master, how He intended to dispose of *him*. " Lord, says he, and " what shall *this* man do?" Or, what is to be *his* lot and destiny? To this our Saviour replies in the words of the text, " if " I will that he tarry till I come, what is " that to thee? Follow thou me."

## SERMON XV.

The anfwer, you may obferve, is in no wife adapted to the queftion: it is adapted however to a better purpofe. The queftion was a matter of mere curiofity in which St. Peter had no concern, and therefore deferved no anfwer. The difpofition which moved him to make the enquiry was fuch as ought to be checked, and therefore our Saviour, in his wifdom and goodnefs, framed his reply accordingly. For the natural import of the anfwer is a plain reproof to his unneceffary inquifitivenefs, prying into a fubject which it was of no ufe to him in the world to know; and an intimation, that the great and chief thing which fhould engage his attention, was to prepare himfelf for the difcharge of his own duty.

This rebuke applied here to a fingle inftance, may juftly be extended to many more

more of a similar nature. For many more such instances there are. *We* have our curiosity as well as the *Apostle*; and *our* curiosity, like *his*, often runs into unnecessary points. How many speculations are formed, and how many questions are agitated among Christians, that have no regard to their real concern? Speculations and questions that fall directly under the censure of my text. For to those who are engaged in them it may very properly be said: " Whether these things be *so* or *so* " what is that to you? they make no part " of your concern: attend to your own " affairs; learn your duty, and fulfil it." In this view the words are of general use; and carry in them a warm admonition to *all* Christians, not to indulge needless curiosity in the dark mysteries of the Gospel; but to study and apply themselves to those *practical* precepts which lead to holiness

and

and a good life. All things indeed contained in the Gospel—the doctrines as well as the precepts of it are subservient to piety; and of consequence should be carefully studied. But the misfortune is, that, not content with what is written, we push our enquiries beyond Revelation; and perplex ourselves with abstruse matters which are too high for us; matters that we are not concerned to know, at least in the degree we presumptuously aim at. Now, to dissuade men from so perverse a conduct, need we say any more than, what with truth may be said, that most of those mysterious points we have in search, are surrounded with such darkness, that we cannot, with all our endeavours, attain to the knowledge of them? They lie far above, beyond the reach of our comprehension; and therefore inaccessible to our present faculties. The mysterious union

of

of the blessed Trinity; that of two natures in the person of CHRIST; the necessity of our Saviour's incarnation and sufferings; the secret œconomy of Providence; the method of divine grace; the state of departed souls; and the particular nature of those rewards and punishments which await us in the other world: these, and such points as these, we may perhaps wish to know, and labour to discover. Yet all our wishes and labours will never carry us with any certainty beyond the limits of Revelation. The light from above is our only safe guide in these matters. So far as this leads, we go upon sure ground; but as soon as it forsakes us we are lost and bewildered. Every discovery we attempt further is mere guess-work; gives no satisfaction, and is of no use. Would indeed be of no use, though actually acquired. For these secret things belong not unto us,

but

but unto the LORD our GOD : and therefore it is, that they are kept fecret. What relates to ourfelves, the things we are concerned to *believe* and to *do*, are all clearly revealed, and lie level to the moft common capacities.

To inftance firft in what regards belief. Surely it requires no mighty depth for any man to convince himfelf, that what the GOD of truth has revealed, fhould readily be embraced : that what he has expreffed in the language of men, fhould be taken and underftood according to the meaning of that language ; that if there are fome things which exceed the powers of our reafon, that they were defigned to exercife our Faith : and that it is ftill rational to believe them, as they come from GOD, though we cannot thoroughly comprehend them. For the true and proper foundation

## SERMON XV. 319

of Faith is not the quality or clearnefs of the thing revealed; but the teftimony and authority of the perfon who reveals it. Faith always implies obfcurity in its object. When a thing is clear, and perfectly known, it is no longer believed. For knowledge excludes belief and fwallows it up, juft in the fame manner as fruition or enjoyment abforbs hope. Thefe obfervations and fentiments naturally arife in every confiderate breaft. And they who approach the Scriptures with thefe fentiments and impreffions, will find no great difficulty in believing thofe articles of faith which are there propofed to them.

They will find ftill lefs in what relates to practice; in affenting to the rules and precepts delivered. For, the virtues they enjoin are fo conformable to our notions of God and goodnefs, fo agreeable to the

dic-

dictates of our reason and conscience, that, if we are free from the influence of prejudice and passion, we cannot but approve them. If in consequence of this approbation, we actually quit the road of vice, and direct our course in pursuit of virtue, we shall daily perceive more clearly the wisdom of the dispensation under which we live. For this is a certain truth, that the practice of Religion is a great help to our more complete knowledge of it. It is so, as it engages our attention to that which is good. It is so, as it keeps the mind candid and sincere, and open to conviction. It is so, as it entitles us to the blessing of God on our honest endeavours, whose goodness will never suffer those, who serve and seek him with their whole heart, to err for want of knowledge. If they are disposed to do his will, they shall know of the doctrine, so much at

least

least as is necessary to make them wise unto salvation.

If this will not satisfy us, but our curiosity still pants after higher knowledge; and would fain enter into the hidden mysteries of the Gospel, then let me remind you further, of the absolute unprofitableness of such enquiries. They can turn to no account. Suppose our Saviour had informed St. Peter what was to become of his beloved disciple, how would he have been the better for it, or what advantage could he have reaped from it? If such information could be of no service in *his* case, what end I beseech you, could be served, or what benefit attained in *ours*, were we all admitted into a clear view of those mysterious truths which are locked up from us? How would Religion then be in a better state than it is at present, or ourselves in a condition to be better men?

Under the present state of Religion we are informed, and we understand, that there are three persons jointly concerned in the work of our Redemption. The Father ordained the plan; the Son graciously accomplished it; and the Holy Ghost enables us to fulfil those conditions, which are requisite to secure the benefits of it. We are moreover informed for our comfort, that each of them is equal to what he has assumed, because each of them is God. But how these *three* persons are but *one* God, we comprehend not. And did we comprehend it, how would that knowledge contribute to render us either more grateful or more obedient, than we ought to be on the present system? Our gratitude and obedience are founded, not on the mystery

of

of the Trinity, which we may never know, but on the things that have been done for us, and are required of us. These we know full well: and if we act and do according to these things happy are we.

By the light at present afforded us we understand, that the HOLY SPIRIT is ever ready to strengthen our infirmities, and to help us forwards in our duty; and though we are not acquainted with the method of his operations, yet how can that either render his grace the less effectual, or our obstinacy in resisting it the less sinful?

In the same manner we understand, that there are great rewards appropriated to the righteous, and great punishments to the wicked, in another life; and though we know not the precise nature of these rewards and punishments what they are,

or

or wherein they confift—yet is it not fufficient in all reafon to influence our conduct, that we know, as we do know, that the one will make us extremely happy, and the other extremely miferable?

What has been faid of thefe, may eafily be applied to other points; and plainly fhews, that the myfteries of Religion are no detriment or difadvantage to it: fhews indeed that they ferve to fupport its dignity and power. I appeal to every man's breaft, whether we fhould entertain the fame awful impreffions of the divine Majefty, if the perfections of his nature and the difpenfations of his providence, were only fuch as we could clearly fee, and perfectly account for. Whether it does not heighten our notion, and raife the value of man's redemption, that it was effected in fuch a miraculous manner—in a manner not

not only beyond example, but even beyond our comprehenſion. Had theſe things been leſs ſublime we ſhould, it is true, have known them better; but the more you lower them, to bring them nearer to our capacities, the more you weaken the power of them upon our affections. And the leſs power they have on our affections, the leſs ſerviceable are they to the purpoſes of religion. For it is the whole buſineſs of religion to influence our affections; to make us ardent in our love to GOD, and zealous in our obedience to him. To this end Revelation, as it is, is excellently adapted. We are debarred from no knowledge that is requiſite to engage our piety and wonder, and yet have not ſo much as would deſtroy our reverence and humility. Between the light and the darkneſs we are kept in a due poize: and we have reaſon to conclude, that it would not have been better, probably not near fo well, if either more had been difcovered to us, or more had been concealed from us. With this therefore we ought to be content:

Efpecially when we confider further, that fuch bold enquiries into hidden things are not only unprofitable, but dangerous too:—of fatal confequence, many times, to the perfons who make them; to others who are feduced and corrupted by them; and to the caufe of Religion in general.

The perfons who purfue fuch curious fpeculations are themfelves great fufferers by them; becaufe they take them off from more ufeful fubjects. We are fent into the world, not fo much to furnifh our heads with knowledge, as to improve our hearts in virtue. The knowledge of our duty

duty, which is all we really want, lies in a small compass, and by the help of Revelation is easily attained; but the practice of it is so difficult and extensive, that it requires all our time and all our pains to carry us through it, and make us perfect in it. Our passions and appetites are hard to be subdued. The attacks of temptations are hard to be resisted. Much labour and diligence are necessary to raise us to any height in virtue: and when raised on high, nothing less than constant watchfulness can secure us from relapsing into vice. Was there then no other inconvenience attending these airy disquisitions, than that they draw us aside from our main business— the improvement of our lives—yet surely that alone is sufficient in conscience to deter us from the pursuit of them. But our curiosity in this respect is productive of further mischiefs. It tinctures the mind

Y 4           very

very strongly with various sorts of vices. It puffs up, and fills us with pride. It renders us captious and assuming; "doting "about questions and strifes of words, "whereof cometh envy, contention, rail- "ings, evil surmisings and perverse dis- "putings." All which, as they are of infinite ill consequence to ourselves; so are they matter of great scandal to others, who will be induced thereby to think religion a thing of indifference, and to shelter their vices under our disputes.

And can we possibly wrong Religion more, than by turning it thus from a rule of life into a matter of science? As if men were better or worse in proportion to what they *know*, and not in proportion to what they *do*. But be your knowledge what it will; can knowledge save you? It is, like Faith without works, dead and insignificant.

nificant. Happiness depends on practice. For he only, who doth the will of GOD, has the promise of being rewarded by him. Know and believe ever so much of the doctrines of Religion, yet all your knowledge and belief, unless adorned by a good life, will at last, like the faith of devils, serve but to make you fear and tremble.

Let this then check your inquisitiveness into speculative subjects, and fix your attention to those that are practical. CHRIST has made you wise enough, and strong enough, unto salvation. He has revealed what you ought to believe: He has told you what you ought to practise: And he gives you abilities to act accordingly. Study therefore the rules of your duty: press upon yourselves the motives to it; and by the influence of those motives endeavour earnestly to accomplish and fulfil it.

Such

Such a diligent obfervance of the plain preceptive parts of Chriftianity will bring in to us immediately a vaft and prefent profit—a profit that will grow daily upon our hands, and fully reward us for our trouble. It will correct the depravity of our nature; reform our difpofitions; eradicate our vices; and improve our virtues. It will operate to our own perfection, and the benefit of all around us. And God, who is a lover of men, thinks himfelf much better ferved when we are ufeful and exemplary to the age we live in, than when we purfue the higheft and moft fubtle fpeculations. This is to follow Christ; for he went about doing good; and hath given us an example that we fhould tread in his fteps. This God hath fhewed us to be our duty. For "what "doth the Lord require of us, but to do "juftly, and to love mercy, and to walk
"hum-

" humbly before him." Herein therefore let us more particularly exercife ourfelves. For after all our enquiries, we fhall be forced at laft to agree with Solomon in this conclufion—" That to fear " God, and keep his commandments is " the whole concern of man." The only thing that can give us comfort here—and the only thing that can make us happy hereafter.

SERMON

# SERMON XVI.

# SERMON XVI.[*]

PSALM xviii.—3.

THE OVERFLOWINGS OF UNGODLINESS MADE ME AFRAID.

THE civil condition of every state, whether good or bad, has always been observed to maintain a regular and exact correspondence with the moral conduct and character of its inhabitants. The nature of

[*] This Sermon was preached upon a fast-day during the American war.

things and the decree of God have so closely connected them together, that the one is invariably determined by the other. " When the people are righteous, the nation is exalted: when they become vicious, it is brought low."

Upon this principle, confirmed to him by the experience of ages, the Royal Prophet, when he saw his subjects disavowing their allegiance, and acting a wicked and rebellious part, could not help expressing his fears of those dreadful miseries, which so impious a conduct was likely to bring both on the kingdom and themselves. Such " overflowings of ungodliness made him afraid." And indeed well they might. For vices of every degree have always an ill effect on the public: and the higher they rise, the more ruinous the consequences. When impiety therefore breaks its bounds,

## SERMON XVI.

bounds, and threatens to overflow the land; all, who are expofed to the fury of the inundation, have great reafon to be afraid: have great reafon to guard againſt their danger; and to unite their endeavours for the common fafety, by checking and diverting its deſtructive courfe.

That popular vices not only may, but actually did among feveral nations, rife up to fuch an enormous height, we are fully affured by the concurrent teſtimony of ancient hiſtories. What the caufes were, that chiefly contributed to this notorious wickednefs, we are not always told: nor does it concern us much to know. This, however, let us carefully remark, that the very fame hiſtories, which give us an account of the manifold vices thofe nations practifed, give us likewife as clear an account of the manifold calamities they con-

fequently

fequently fuffered. And let this remark excite us, as it ought, ferioufly to reflect on our own conduct; and examine, how *we* are really circumftanced in this refpect.

When we come to enter on this important examination, the following queftion will naturally occur—" are we better than they?" Better, doubtlefs, we ought to be, becaufe we enjoy greater advantages. The fuperior excellency of our religion fhould, in reafon, make us more excellent in our lives: and the mighty bleffings we have been favoured with, fhould have kept us fteadfaft in our religious obedience to that gracious Being, from whofe liberal bounty they originally flowed.

That God, who has fhewed himfelf fo peculiarly beneficent to us, ought, furely,

to

to be adored by us, with peculiar reverence, and holy zeal. But have we that awful veneration for Him, which his Majesty claims?—that inward piety towards Him, which his goodnefs demands? Are we always careful to give Him the honour due unto his name; and to worfhip Him with holy worfhip? Are we always attentive to what He commands; and diligent in the obfervance of his righteous injunctions? How comes his name then to be fo commonly, and fo wantonly profaned? How comes his fanctuary then to be fo little frequented; to be indeed fo forfaken, fo defolate, as it is? How come his laws then to be fo flightly regarded, fo prefumptuoufly defpifed, fo daringly violated, as we know they are?

Thefe, alas! are manifeft figns of the decay of piety: woful indications of the

want

want of Religion. But when once Religion and the fear of God are thus unhappily thrown afide; then will inevitably fpring up in their ftead diforder, confufion, and every evil work. This all the former ages experienced: and this we now experience ourfelves.

For, ever fince we have learned to forget our God, and to neglect his religion and worfhip; with what fhamelefs front have licentioufnefs and debauchery, intemperance and luxury, been ftalking through the land? Thefe arrogant vices foon introduced a kindred troop of others, as miniftering fervants to fupply their demands: Such are fraud and injuftice, rapine and violence, cruelty and oppreffion, treachery and deceit. Behind thefe we may obferve a confufed group of leffer vices, extremely injurious to the welfare of fociety, society, as well as displeasing to the purity of GOD: such as falsehood and perfidiousness, pride and envy, malice and revenge, slander and detraction, uncharitableness, selfishness, and discontent.

View this picture, this portrait of the nation, and own it to be just: view the original, and be afraid. For with how great and reasonable an apprehension must every serious man look on this state of things, who considers the grievous and miserable consequences that must naturally attend it!

It has ever been observed, that when profaneness and irreligion have prevailed among any people, all civil crimes have abounded likewise, to the great danger and detriment of the state. And how indeed should it possibly be otherwise? For when men once cease to " fear GOD," it cannot be expected, that they should long continue, either to " love the brotherhood," or to " honour the king." And when brotherly love and mutual benevolence no longer subsist among them, what room is there left for good faith and mutual confidence? And when mutual confidence is destroyed, must not every one live in constant distrust of every other; and think himself obliged to be perpetually on his guard against their violence, or their deceit? But when the wild lusts and raging passions of corrupt nature are let loose to their several pursuits, who knows from what quarter, or in what measure, insults and injuries may fall upon him? This only the good man knows, and this he sincerely laments, that such general disorders, though they hurt him much, must injure the community infinitely more: must disturb its peace, and destroy its harmony;

mony : muft weaken its powers, and fruftrate its defigns : muft fubject its authority to be defpifed abroad, becaufe found to be fo little refpected at home.

When a nation comes to this pafs, how juftifiable are our fears for its welfare, if we confider only thefe deftructive confequences, which naturally refult from its wickednefs and corruption? But how much higher muft our concern rife, when we confider it moreover, as expofed to the vengeance of an offended God?

For, though every vice, is, by the eftablifhed laws of nature, conftantly attended with fome immediate punifhment; yet thefe natural and ordinary penalties are not the whole that is always due and ordained to our crimes. When they become general,

general, they become more malignant; and confequently deferve more fignal inflictions. Private fins may fafely be referved to the final doom; but it is highly expedient on many accounts, that general and public fins fhould meet with general and public punifhment. And indeed, have they not always met with it? Look at the generations of old, and fee; confult the ages that are paft, and obferve; whether any ftate or kingdom, overrun with impiety, vice and immorality, was ever fuffered to go unpunifhed? The chief accounts of former times, what are they, but fo many declared inftances of GOD's awful and avenging power, exercifed on finful and incorrigible nations? For when they obftinately perfifted in evil courfes, and wickednefs became prevalent among them, He took the government into his own hands, and, by the immediate interpofition of his fupreme

## SERMON XVI.

preme authority, chaſtiſed them with viſible and diſtinguiſhed ſtrokes of reſentment.

With what impreſſions of terrour then muſt every one, who believes in a GOD and a providence, behold himſelf in the midſt of a land, whoſe morals have for ſome time been extremely depraved; and, notwithſtanding repeated warnings, are continually proceeding from bad to worſe? He knows, that the LORD, who hateth iniquity, "will certainly viſit for theſe things:" and therefore his fears may juſtly be alarmed, leſt the ſame calamities ſhould be inflicted on his own, as were formerly inflicted, in the like caſe, on other corrupt and impenitent nations.

After what manner the Almighty may exert himſelf; or what evils we are to eſtimate

timate as immediate inftances of his divine refentment, we cannot prefume to fay. But this however we may fay with certainty—and this our prefent fituation leads us ferioufly to reflect upon—that, when any nation becomes remarkably corrupt and immoral, it is one mode of divine punifhment, firft to divide it againft itfelf; and then to make the divided powers mutual fcourges to each other. Hear what the Lord fays by his Prophet to the frequently admonifhed, but unrepenting, Egypt. " I have mingled a perverfe fpi-
" rit in the midft thereof. And I will fet
" the Egyptians againft the Egyptians:
" and they fhall fight every one againft his
" brother, and every one againft his neigh-
" bour; city againft city; and kingdom
" againft kingdom: and Egypt fhall
" fall."

# SERMON XVI.

To whatever cause then we may be disposed in *politics* to attribute our dissentions and national calamities; in *reason* and *religion* it would be most prudent to ascribe them to our accumulated national sins: and consequently, to seek their removal by unfeigned national repentance. To such repentance we are strongly pressed by various and weighty reasons. It is one of the most effectual means to compose and allay our contentions: one of the most effectual means to relieve us from the evils we labour under: one of the most effectual means to restore to us our lost happiness. We have never yet gained any thing by our vices: by our repentance we may gain much. Our vices indeed we must renounce, if we are duly sensible of their fatal tendency. And yet, wholly insensible we cannot be. For the natural consequences of our sins, and the superadded punishment in-

inflicted on them, have appeared plainly for some time—in the diftreffes and calamities of private life; and in the burdens, diforders, and uneafineffes of the public: and now, in the additional increafe that is made to our enemies; and in the additional expence we muft neceffarily be at, to maintain ourfelves againft their efforts.

What fuccefs we fhall finally meet with in the courfe of this lengthened conteft, He only knows, who knows all things. We may vainly boaft, that we have ftrength for the war: but our wifdom would be, to fecure inftantly, *his* aid, in whofe hands are the iffues of it, by humble contrition and fincere penitence. Then may we fafely affume confidence. For if we make " the " LORD our refuge and ftrength, we fhall " be fure to find him a very prefent help " in all our troubles."

Preffed,

Pressed, as we are, by such weighty considerations, let us accordingly endeavour to recall and revive the genuine spirit of true religion. Let us be careful to reverence God, in his name, in his sabbaths, in his sanctuary. Let us use all diligence to reform our tempers, to correct our failures and to improve our virtues. Let us estimate life, not as a scene of dissipation and thoughtlessness—not as a scene of pleasure and amusements—but, as what it really is, a state of probation and trial; where we must necessarily perfect ourselves in goodness, if we mean to secure either present comfort, or future peace and eternal happiness.

Thus reason directs us to act: and here interest coincides with reason, and pleads for reformation with redoubled force. We are apt to complain, that the times are bad,
and

and our profpect gloomy. " Would we then fee better times? Let us efchew evil, and do good: let us feek peace, and enfue it. For the eyes of the Lord are over the righteous; and his ears are open unto all their prayers: and no good thing will he ever withhold from them that lead a godly life."

If then we have any real concern for the welfare and profperity of our country; let us now prove it, not by our words, but by our actions: by concurring to ftop the contagion of fin, and the overfpreading deluge of iniquity: by making ourfelves exemplars of virtue, and promoters of every good. Every degree of virtuous improvement will contribute fomething to the benefit of the ftate. The more perfect our amendment, the brighter will be our profpect, and the greater our hope. And

would

would but this national humiliation produce, what is unqueſtionably meant it ſhould produce, a national reformation; then might we boldly ſay in the language of the Prophets :—

"Aſſociate yourſelves, O ye people, and
"ye ſhall be broken in pieces: take coun-
"ſel together, and it ſhall come to nought:
"ſpeak the word, and it ſhall not ſtand:
"for GOD is with us. Sanctify therefore
"the LORD of hoſts; and let him be your
"fear; and let him be your dread: and he
"will be for a ſanctuary unto you.—For
"GOD will ſave Sion, and build the cities
"of Judah. The poſterity alſo of his
"ſaints ſhall inherit it; and they that love
"his name ſhall dwell therein. Their
"children ſhall continue; and their ſeed
"ſhall be eſtabliſhed before him." Amen!

FINIS.

# SUBSCRIBERS NAMES.

### A.

ARMAGH His Grace the Archbishop of. 2 copies.
Abbot Mrs. Highbury Place.
Abel Mrs. Edmonton. 2 copies.
Adams Mrs. Hatton Garden.
Adderley Thomas Esq. Stoke-Newington.
Adderley, Esq. Doctors-Commons.
Adeane Mrs. Robert.
A. E.
Alder Mr. Gilbert, Savage-Gardens.
Alers Mr. William.
Allen Thomas, Esq. Edmonton. 2 copies.
Allen Alexander Peter Esq. Mill-Green House, Essex.
Allen Mr.
Allen Dr.
Allen William, Esq. Clifford's Inn.
Allen Thomas, Esq. ditto.
Allen Edward, Esq. ditto.
Allnutt John, Esq. Mark Lane.
Allnutt Richard, Esq. South-Park.

Allwood Rev. P. Wandfworth.
Amphlett Rev. Dr.
Anderdon I. P. Efq. Highbury-Grove.
Anderfon James, Efq.
Anderfon James, Jun. Efq. [Coleman, &c.
Andrews Rev. Townfend. Rector of St. Katharine-
Andrews Rev. Robert-Townfend.
Andrey Mrs. Swindon.
Ange Mrs. Glocefter-Street.
Anguin Capt.
Appach ——, Efq.
Arden Mr. Southgate.
Arnold William, Efq.
Afhnefs Thomas, Efq. Clapham.
Afkey Rev. Henry, Yarlington.
Atkinfon Mr.
Atkinfon Mrs. Norwood. 2 copies.
Atwood Mr. and Mrs. Taviftock-Street. 5 copies.
Auftin Mrs. Ormond Street.
Auftin James, Efq. Cooper's Row.
Auftin Mrs. Hackney.
Aynfcombes Mifs, Mortlake.
Aynfworth Mrs. Bloomfbury-Square.
Ayton Mrs. Bruce-Caftle, Tottenham.

B.

Barrington Hon. Mrs. Cavendifh-Square,.
Barrington Hon. Admiral.
Barrington Hon. Daines.

Babington

## SUBSCRIBERS NAMES.

Babington Dr.
Bacon John, Esq. First-Fruits Office.
Bacon Miss.
Baker Rev. Slade.
Baker Jacob, Esq.
Baker John, Esq. Snaresbrook.
Baker William, Esq. ditto.
Baker Miss, ditto.
Bamston Mrs. M. Bath.
Banks William, Esq. Winstanley. 2 copies.
Banks Mr. R.
Barker Mrs. Ann, Tottenham.
Barker Mrs, East Sheen.
Barlow Rev. F. G. Tooting.
Barnard Daniel, Esq. Clapham.
Barnard Rev. C. Langham, Suffolk.
Barnardiston Nathanael, Esq.
Barrett Mr. Bath.
Barronneau Mrs.
Barrow Taylor. Esq.
Barstow Mrs.
Batley Jeremiah, Esq. Lambs-Conduit Street.
Battin ——, Esq. East-Marden, Sussex.
Battin Mrs. ditto.
Battin Mrs. Mary, Compton.
Bax Mrs. Feversham.
Baxter Rev. George, Tower-Hill.
Baxter James, Esq.
Bayford Mrs. Lambs-Conduit-Street.
Beachcroft Mrs. Tottenham.
Beachcroft Samuel, Esq. Little St. Helens, 2 copies.

Bean Mrs. Richmond.
Beardfworth Mifs.
Beatfon Mr. John, Cateaton-Street.
Beckingham Rev.—— Rector of Hardres, Kent.
Bedell Mr. Dartford. 2 copies.
Begbie A. Efq. New-Broad-Street.
Belchier Mrs. Great-Ruffel-Street.
Bel! Rev. Dr. Fellow of St. John's Oxford, and Chaplain to the Factory, at Oporto. 4 copies.
Bell Mr. R. B. Cooper's Row.
Bell Mifs. Eltham.
Bell Rev. R. B.—LL. B. New-college, Oxford.
Bellis Mr. William, Edmonton.
Belward Rev. Dr. Mafter of Caius College, Cambridge.
Bennet P. Efq. Barton, Suffolk.
Bennet Mrs. St. Edmond's Bury.
Benfon Mifs. Grofvenor Street.
Berdmore Rev. Dr. Scrope, Warden of Merton College Oxford, 2 copies.
Berkley Rev. Dr. Writtle, Effex.
Bernal I. I. Efq. Fitzroy Square.
Berwick Mrs. Hallow-Houfe, Worcefter.
Bethune Rev. G. M. Rector of Wanftrow.
Bettefworth Mrs. The Hide, Herts.
Beverley Cornet, W. R.
Biker Rev. Thomas. M. A. Culworth, Northampton.
Bing George, Efq. M. P.
Bingley Thomas, Jun. Efq. Birching Lane.
Birch Rev. Thomas. LL.B. Fellow of St. John's, Oxford.
Birch Mrs. Thomas, Bond-Street.

Bird

## SUBSCRIBERS NAMES.

Bird Thomas, Efq.
Bird Mrs. Bath. 2 copies.
Bird Mifs.    ditto.
Bifhop Rev. William, Henftridge.
Blache I. T. Efq.
Blackburne John, Efq. Bufh-Hill. 3 copies.
Blackburne Mrs.        ditto.
Blackburne Mifs.       ditto.
Blackburne Mifs. Frances, ditto.
Blackburne John, Jun. Efq. ditto.
Blackburne Henry-Stephenfon, Efq. ditto.
Blackburne George Hanway.    ditto.
Blackburne Edward Berens.    ditto.
Blackburne Mrs. Park-Street, Weftminfter.
Blackman John-Lucie, Efq. Craven-Street.
Blackman Mrs.          ditto.
Blackwood Shovell, Efq. Serle-Street.
Blair Colonel, Stratford Place.
Blake Mrs.  Iflington.
Blake Mrs.
Blakifton Rev. George F——B. D. Fellow of St. John's Oxford.
Blayney Rev. Dr. Regius Profeffor of Hebrew and Canon of Chrift Church, Oxford.
Blizard William, Efq. Devonfhire-Square.
Blofeld Thomas, Efq. Temple.
Bloxam Matthew, Efq. M. P. Southwark.
Boddam Rawfon-Hart, Efq. Capell-Houfe.
Boddam Mrs.          ditto.
Boddington Thomas, Efq. Clapton 2 copies.

Boddington

Boddington Mrs. Samuel, Southgate, 2 copies.
Bond Rev. I. Suffolk.
Bonham Henry, Esq.
Bonham Mrs. Hatton-Street.
Bosanquet Samuel, Esq. Forest-House, Walthamstow. 2 copies.
Boucher Rev. Richard, Bright-Waltham, Berks.
Boucher John, Esq. Edmonton, 5 copies.
Bowen Mr. Thomas.
Bowles Miss. Wanstead-House, Essex.
Bowman John, Esq..
Boyd Mrs. Putney-Hill.
Bradbury Rev. William, Saling, Essex.
Bragg Mr. Stephen. Edmonton.
Brant Mrs. Highbury-Terrace.
Brazier Mrs. Cooper's Row.
Bredel Peter, Esq. Spital-Square.
Breese Mr. Mrs. and Family, Cooper's-Row. 5 copies.
Brent Mrs. Adelphi.
Bricdale ———, Esq. Court-House, Taunton.
Bricdale John, Esq. ditto.
Brickwood Nathanael, Esq. St. Mary Axe.
Bridges Mrs. Canterbury.
Bridges John, Esq. Tooting.
Bridges George, Esq.
Bright John, Esq. Tooting.
Broadly Mrs.
Brockfopp Mr. Edward, Savage-Gardens.
Brocus Mrs. Upper-Grosvenor Street.
Brooks Miss, Norwich

Broughton

Broughton B. Efq.
Brown Mrs, Cooper's Row.
Brown Mr. Edward]
Brown Mr. Timothy, St. Mary Hill.
Browne James, Efq. 3 copies.
Browne Mrs. Cheapfide.
Browning William, Efq.
Bryant Jacob, Efq. Upper Norton Street. 2 copies.
Buckner Rev. Dr.
Bulcock James, Efq. St. Margaret's Hill.
Bunny Mrs. Bath, 2 copies.
Burchall —— Efq. Pig-Street.
Burlton Mifs, Edmonton.
Burlton Mifs Ann, ditto.
Burminfter —— Efq. Bifhopfgate-Street.
Burnfide Andrew, Efq. Bourn-houfe, Bexley, Kent.
Bufhnan Mrs. Tottenham.
Bufk, Mrs. Leeds.
Butterworth, Mr. Bufh-Hill.
Butterworth Mifs, ditto.,
Buxton Mrs. Mortimer-Street.
Buxton —— Efq. Mincing Lane.

## C

Canterbury his Grace the Archbifhop of. 10 copies.
Clarke Lady, Edmonton.
Canterbury Rev. the Dean and Chapter of. 2 copies.
Cade Philip, Efq. Bath,]

Cade

Cade Mrs. ditto.
Cain Mrs. Stapleford-Tawney, Eſſex.
Calrow Joſeph, Eſq. St, Mary-Hill.
Calverley Thomas, Eſq. Ewell, 5 copies.
Calverley Mrs. ditto.
Calverley Thomas, jun. Eſq. ditto, 2 copies.
Carne C. I. Eſq.
Carr Rev. C. Twickenham.
Cartier John Eſq. Bedgebury, Kent.'
Cattley Stephen, Eſq. Park-place, Camberwell.
Cawne ——— Eſq. Mercers-Hall.
Chalic Mr.
Champion Alexander, Eſq. Wincheſter-Str. 10 copies.
Champion Benjamin, Eſq. New-Broad-Street.
Champion Miſs, ditto.
Chapman George, Eſq.
Chapman Sands, Eſq.
Chapman Mr. William, Lothbury.
Charleton Mrs. White-Friars, Gloceſter.
Cherry George, Eſq. Devonſhire-Street, Queen-ſquare.
Chatfield Mr. John.
Chatfield, Mrs. Cooper's Row.
Chauncey, Charles Snell, Eſq. Theobald's.
Clark Mrs. Norwich.
Clark, George, Eſq.
Clark Mr. Charles.
Clarke Rev. Thomas, M. A. Rector of Ickenham.
Clarke Mrs.
Clarke I. Eſq. Store-Street, Bedford-Square.
Clarke W. S. ditto.

           Clarke

Clarke J. Calvert, Efq. Barbican.
Clarke Mifs. Dean-Street, Audley-fquare.
Clarke William, Efq. Tottenham.
Clarke Mrs. Ditto.
Clarke Mr. Anthony. Throgmorton-Street.
Clarke Mr. William. Gracechurch-Street.
Claxton William, Efq. Enfield.
Claxton John, Efq. Shirley, near Croydon.
Claxton Mrs.
Cock Mr.
Cole Charles, Efq. Southgate.
Colkett Daniel, Efq. Hackney.
Collier Mr. John.
Collier Mrs. Jane.
Colfon John, Efq. Crutched Friars.
Complin Mr. Enfield.
Coney Rev. William. Rector of Breamore, Hants. 5 copies.
Coney Mrs.
Coney Rev. T. Batcomb.
Coney Bicknell, Efq. Leadenhall-Street, 2 copies.
Conybeare Rev. Dr. Rector of St. Botolph, Bifhopfg.
Cook Rev. Dr. Dean of Ely.
Cook Rev. Wafhbourne. Rector of Hardwick, Bucks.
2 copies.
Cooke Rev. Dr. Fellow of Oriel College, Oxford.
Cooper Rev. —— Barton, Suffolk.
Copeland Gabriel, Efq. Clapham.
Corbett Mr. Peter, New-Street, Bifhopfgate.
Core Mrs. Tottenham.
Corkran Lewis, Efq. Gower-Street.
Cornthwaite Rev. Thomas. Vicar of Hackney.

Cornthwate Mr. Bank.
Cotton Rev. R. H. Enfield.
Cottrell Rev. Charles, Jeffreys, AM.
Coulthard Mrs.
Courtney Rev. J. Trinity College, Cambridge.
Coward Thomas, Efq. Spargrove.
Cowell John, Efq.
Cowell G. Efq.
Cox Rev. ———. Rector of Acton.
Cox ——— Efq.
Cracherode Rev. ———.
Cranmer Rev. Robert. Rector of Nurfling, Kent.
Cranmer Mrs. Martha.
Crefpigney Mrs. Camberwell.
Crifp Mrs. Stoke-Newington.
Croft ———, Efq. Oporto. 2 copies.
Crofts Mifs. Bath.
Crofby Mr. Robert. St. John Street.
Crofby Robert, Efq. Hoxton-Square.
Crofby Mrs. Chatham-Place.
Croffe Richard, Efq.
Croughton William, Efq. Camberwell.
Croughton Mrs. Clapham.
Crowther P. W. Efq. Guildhall.
Cumming Mifs.
Currie Mark, Efq. Bloomfbury.
Currie Ifaac, Efq. Cornhill.
Curteis William, Efq. Camberwell.
Curtis Mr. Alderman. M. P. 2 copies.
Curtis Timothy, Efq. Hackney.
Cufack Chriftopher, Efq. Rathaldon-Caftle, Meath, Ireland.
Durham,

## D.

Durham the Hon. and Rt. Rev. the Ld. Bp. of. 50 copies.
Ducie Lord. Dover-Street, Piccadilly.
Dale Dr. Union-Court, Broad-Street.
Dalton John, Esq. Pitcombe.
Dampier Rev. Dr. Dean of Rochester.
Dampier Henry, Esq. Bloomsbury-Square.
Daranda Mrs. Mary. Putney.
Daranda Mrs. Henrietta. ditto.
D'Aranda Rev. Peter, M. A. Vicar of Great Burstead, Essex.
Darby John, Esq. Cambridge-Heath, Hackney.
Darell Edward, Esq.
Darell Robert, Esq.
Dauncey Mrs. Hart-Street, Bloomsbury.
Davidson Mrs. 6 copies.
Davies Rev. Dr. Provost of Eton.
Davies Mrs. Frances. 2 copies.
Dawe Hill, Esq. Ditchet.
Dawson Edward, Esq.
Dawson Mrs.
Dawson William, Esq. Ampthill, Bedfordshire.
Dawson Mrs.
Deacon Mr. James.
Dealtry Miss. 2 copies.
Dearman Rev. Henry. Uxbridge. 10 copies.
Delamars Mrs. Theobald's, Cheshunt. 10 copies.
Derby Mrs.
De Visme Philip Nathanael, Esq. 5 copies.
De Visme, Mrs.

De Vifme ——— Philip, Efq;
De Vifme Gerard, Efq.
De Vifme Mifs.
De Vifme Mifs Louifa.
De Vifme Mifs Harriet.
De Vifme Gerard, Efq. Grofvenor-Square,
Dewar Edward, Efq. Clapham,
Dewar Mrs.
Dickerfon Mrs. Tottenham,
Dickinfon John, Efq.
Dixon William, Efq.
Dixon Mrs. Eltham.
Dixon Mr. Charles. Savage-Gardens,
Docwra Mr. Thomas, Ware
Dodd Rev. ———,
Dolly Mifs.
Dolignon Mrs.
Donaldfon William, Efq. 10 copies.
Dorrien George, Efq. Margaret-Street, CavendifhSquare,
Dorfet Mrs. Brook-Street.
Douglas Mr.
Dove Rev. I. Ipfwich,
Dowel Mr.
Dow.. Mrs.
Downing Rev. Bladen.
Downing M. Hackney.
D. w. Henry-William, Efq. Peckham,
Drape Mr. Thomas. Limehoufe.
Draper Daniel, Efq. St. James's-Street,
Dreaton ———, Efq. Compton, Suffex.

            Drewe

# SUBSCRIBERS NAMES,

Drewe William, Efq. Spring-Gardens.
Dreyer Rev. I. D. Norwich.
Dupha Mrs. Homerton.
Dyfon Mr. John. Union-Street, Borough.

### E.

Eufton Countefs of.?
Ely the Hon. and Right. Rev. E. the Lord Bifhop of.
Eamonfon —, Efq. Bufh-Hill.
Eamonfon Mrs.   ditto.
Eaton Mr. Richard. Little Tower-Street.
Edgar Mrs. Pall-Mall.
Edwards Mr. Archdeacon. Ciiro, Radnorfhire.
Edwards Mr. John. Stratford.
Egerton Rev. —— North-Mims.
Ellice Rev. Robert. Welwyn. 3 copies.
Elliot Mr.
Ellis Mifs. Hoddefdon.
Ellis Thomas, Efq. St. Margaret's Hill.
Ellis Mr. Jofeph. Tooley-Street.
Elwes ——, Efq. Langham, Bury.
Elwin Mr. Fountain. Edmonton.
Enderby ——, Efq.
Enderby C. Efq.
Enderby S. Efq.
Enderby G. Efq.
Englifh Mr. Ifaac. Edmonton.
Evans George, Efq. Baalam, Clapham.

Evans

Evans George, Esq. Borough.
Evans Percival, Esq. ditto.
Evans Rev. Michael. Acton.
Evans Mrs. — Ty-Mawr, Merionethshire.
Eveleigh Rev. Dr. Provost of Oriel College Oxford.
   2 copies.
Ewer Mrs. John. Dover.
Eyre Rev. Dr. Prebendary of Glocester.
Eyre James, Esq. St. Mary-Hill.
Eyres Colonel.
Eyres Mrs.

### F.

Forrester Lord.
Fletcher Lady. Southampton-Street.
Faget Mr.
Falconer Mrs. Bath.
Farrer John, Esq.
Farrington Mr. Fowlkes-Buildings.
Farrington Miss.
Farrow Thomas, Esq. Love Lane.
Favence Mr. Abraham. Throgmorton-Street.
Fector John Minet, Esq. Dover.
Felten Mrs. Hackney.
Fenwick Mrs. Flint-House, Greenwich.
Fenwick John, Esq. Milbank-Street, Westminster.
Field Mrs. Edward-Street.
Finch Rev. Dr. Prebendary of Westminster.

Finch

## SUBSCRIBERS NAMES.

Finch Rev. Dr. Fellow of St. John's, Oxford.
Fisher Mrs. Park-Street, Westminster. 5 copies.
Fisher Mrs. Bedford-Square.
Forbes Rev. John, B. D. Fellow of St. John's, Oxford.
Forrest Mrs. Worcester.
Forsteen William, Esq. Lime-Street-Square.
Foster Mrs. Richmond.
Foster Mr. Edward. Walthamstow.
Foster Mr.
Foster Mr. Thomas. Clement's-Lane.
Fothergill Rev. Dr. late Provost of Queen's College Ox.
Foy Mrs.
Francis Mr.
Frankland Mrs. Chichester.
Franklin Mr. Dartford.
Franks Mr. W. Clapham.
Free Rev. E. D. B. D. Fellow of St. John's, Oxford.
Freeman John Esq. Letton, Herefordshire.
Freeman Miss. Twickenham.
French J. B. Esq.
Frewin Richard Esq. Great George-Street, Westminster.
Frith Rev. C. Kentish Town.
Fryer Mr. Taplow.

## G.

Gordon Lady Louisa.
Glocester the Right Rev. the Lord Bishop of.
Gamon Sir Richard, Bart. M. P. Minchenden House.
  2 copies.                                              Grey

Grey Sir Henry, Bart.
Gabriel Rev. Dr. Rector of Harlington and Hanworth, Middlesex.
Galhie John, Esq. Spital-Square.
Gardiner Henry, Esq. Wandsworth.
Gardiner Mrs.
Garrett Miss. Stoke-Newington.
Garrow William, Esq. Warwick-Court, Holborn.
Gaskin Rev. Dr. Rector of St. Bene't, Gracechurch.
Gates Miss. Edmonton.
Gearing E. A. Miss. Mile-End, Old-Town.
Gee Osgood, Esq. Lower Seymour Street.
Gellibrand Rev. J. Edmonton.
Gentleman A.
Gentleman A.
Gibbs —— Esq.
Giles Daniel, Esq. Spital-Square, 2 copies.
Gillibrand Thomas, Esq. West-Ham.
Glynn Dr. Fellow of King's College, Cambridge.
Godfrey Mrs. Shaftsbury-House, Kensington.
Golding Henry, Esq. Borough.
Goldsmid Benjamin, Esq.
Goldsmid Mrs. Jessey.
Goldsmid Abraham, Esq.
Goldsmid Asher, Esq.
Gomond Richard, Esq. Bath. 2 copies.
Goodwin Mrs. —— Powick, near Worcester.
Gooch Rev. Dr. Prebendary of Ely.
Gordon Alexander, Esq. Lime-Street.
Goslin George, Esq. Bedford-Square.

         Gosling

## SUBSCRIBERS NAMES.

Gosling J. Esq.
Gosling Francis, Esq.
Gosset Rev. Dr. F. R. S.
Gough Richard Esq. Enfield. 5 copies.
Gough Mrs. Enfield.
Gowland Thomas, Esq.
Graham James, Esq. Lincoln's-Inn. 2 copies.
Gray John, Esq. Winchmore-Hill.
Gray John, Esq. Crausley.
Gray Richard, Esq. Gower-Street, Bedford-Square.
Greene Mrs. Norwich.
Greenland ———, Esq. Carshalton.
Greenland Miss.            ditto.
Grenside John, Esq. Broad-Street. 6 copies.
Grenwollers C. G. Esq. Took's-Court.
Griffith Rev. Griffith. M. A.
Guillemard Isaac, Esq. Tottenham.
Gundry ———, Esq. Richmond.
Gundry Mrs. M.

### H.

Howard Lady. New-Burlington-Street.
Harley Right Hon. Alderman.
Hume Sir Abraham, Bart. Hill-Street, Berkley-Square.
H. F. Mrs.
Hackney Reading Society. 10 copies.
Haggitt Rev. ———. Prebendary of Durham.
Hahn ———, Esq. Wandsworth.
Hale Mr. Greville-Street, Hatton-Garden.
Hale Mrs.

Hall Mr. LL.B. Wadham College, Oxford.
Ham Mr. Spital-Square.
Hamilton Capt.
Hammond Mr. Thomas. Edmonton.
Hand Mr. Archdeacon.
Hankey Robert, Efq. 2 copies.
Hankey Mrs. 2 copies.
Hankey Auguftus, Efq.
Hanfen Mrs. Hackney.
Hardy Mrs. Enfield.
Hardy Rev. Richard. Fellow of Emanuel, Cambridge.
Hare Rev. Robert. Hertfmonceaux-Park, Suffex.
Harman John, Efq. Frederick's-Place.
Harman Jeremiah, Efq. Finfbury-Square.
Harmer Robert, Efq.
Harper Charles, Efq. Poultry.
Harris Mrs. Crefcent, Bath.
Harris Quarles, Efq. Crutched-Friars. 19 copies.
Harris I. Efq. Twyford.
Harris Nathanael, Efq. Peckham.
Harrifon Andrews, Efq. Somerfet-Street, Portman-Square.
Harrifon Mr. I. Tooley-Street.
Harrifon Mifs, Bath.
Hartwell Capt. F. I. Commiffioner of the Victualling-Of.
Hafe Mr. Robert. Clerkenwell.
Hatch James, Efq. 5 copies.
Hatfell James, Efq.
Hatt Rev. Andrew. Aldgate.
Harvey Rev. Thomas. Realeaf, Kent.
Harvey Mrs.—Ickwell, Bury.

            Hawkins

## SUBSCRIBERS NAMES.

Hawkins Samuel, Efq.
Hazard John, Efq.
Hazier Mrs. Turnham-Green.
Heathcote I. E. Efq. Bath. 3 copies.
Heathcote Mrs. A.   ditto. 3 copies.
Heberden Dr. Pall-Mall. 5 copies.
Heddington Mr. William Clement. Spitalfields.
Hencock Mrs. Hamftead-Heath.
Henfhall Mifs. Camberwell.
Henfhaw Robert, Efq.
Henfhaw Mrs.
Hetherington ——. Efq. Buckingham-Street.
Hetherington Mrs. Blackfriars-Road.
Hewghs Mrs. Great George-Street, Weftminfter.
Hey Rev. Dr. Prebendary of Rochefter.
Heyman Henry, Efq. Lincolns-Inn Fields.
Heyman Henry, Jun. Efq. Cateaton-Street.
Hickes Mrs. Oxford.
Hicks I. W. Efq. Bath.
Hicks John, Efq. Chrift-Church, Oxford.
Hill Mrs. Newman-Street.
Hingften Mr. John. Cheapfide.
Hippuff C. Efq. Birchin-Lane.
Hoar George,  Efq. Tower of London. 2 copies.
Hoare Rev. Dr. Principal of Jefus Col. Oxford 2 copies.
Hoare Mrs.
Hobhoufe Henry, Efq. Hatpfden Houfe.
Hockley Mrs. Blackland's-Houfe, Chelfea.
Holden Rev. John. Fellow of Sidney College Cambridge.
Hollingfworth Rev. Nathanael. St. John's College Oxford.
Holloway Mifs. Cornhill.

Holmes

## SUBSCRIBERS NAMES.

Holmes Joseph, Esq. Edmonton. 5 copies.
Holmes Thomas, Esq. Clapham.
Holmes William, Esq. Westcomh-Park.
Holmes Mrs.              ditto.
Holmes William, Esq.
Hopkins ———, Esq.
Hornby Mr. William. Kirkham.
Horsfall Mrs.
Howard Mr. Church-Street, Westminster.
Howell Rev. John. Vicar of Llanarth, Cardiganshire.
Howitt Mrs. Southgate.
Hucks ———. Esq.
Hudson ———. Esq.
Hudson Mr. Tottenham.
Hughes Rev. Thomas. Prebendary of Westminster.
Hughes Rev. Dr. Fellow of Jesus College, Oxford.
Hughes Henry, Esq.
Humphrey Mrs. Wellingborough, Northamptonshire.
Humphreys Mrs. Agnes, Constitution-Row, St. Pancras.
Hunt John, Esq. Coscombe.
Hunt Mr. Joseph.
Hunter Rev. ———. Christ Church, Cambridge.
Hunter Mrs. Gower-Street.
Hunter D. Esq. Blackheath.
Hurry Francis, Esq. Clapton.
Hutchins Mr. Charles. Bowes-Farm.
Huxley Mrs. Edmonton.
Hyatt William, Esq. Shepton-Mallet.

## I.

I. L. Efq. Cooper's Row.
Inglis James, Efq. Mark-Lane. 5 copies.
Ingram Mrs. John-Street, Bedford-Row.
Irving Mr. W. New-Bond-Street.

## J.

James Lady. Upper-Wimpole-Street.
Jackfon Rev. Dr. Canon Refidentiary of St. Paul's. 2 co.
Jackfon James Francis Efq. 3 copies.
Jackfon Thomas, Efq. Camberwell-Terrace.
Jackfon ———. Efq.
Jacobs ———. Efq. Brook-Houfe, Clapton.
James Mr. Elfted.
Jarvis Captain.
Jeffery George, Efq. Peckham. 6 copies.
Jefferys Nathanael, Efq. M. P. Clarges-Street.
Jeffreys Rev. Dr. Canon Refidentiary of St. Pauls.
Jeffreys Mrs. ———. Bath. 2 copies.
Jekyll Mrs. ditto.
Jenkins William, Efq. Shepton-Mallet.
Jenkyns Rev. John. Evercreech.
Jennings Mr. Fenchurch-Street.
Jennings Mrs. ditto.
Jeffopp John, Efq. Waltham Abbey.
Johnfon Godfchall, Efq. Putney-Hill. 2 copies.
Johnfon ———, Efq.

Johnfon

Johnson Mr. Tottenham.
Jones Rev. Owen. Glynn, Merionethshire.
Jones Mrs. Ann. Bath. 5 copies.
Jones Richard, Esq. Took's-Court, Chancery-Lane.
Jones Rev. ———. Cambridge.
Jones Mr.
Jones Mr. E. K. Mark-Lane.
Jones Mrs.              ditto.
Jones Mr. John. Holborn-Hill.
Jones Mr. W. A.    ditto.
Jones Mr. Robert. Edmonton.
Jones Mr. Henry. Mansion-House Street. 2 copies.
Jourdain Major. Upper-Harley-Street.
Jourdain George, Esq. Spital-Square.
Jourdain John, Esq.      ditto.
Jourdain Mrs.            ditto.
Jourdain A. Esq. Great-George-Street.
Jourdain Mrs.            ditto.

### K.

Kallet Henry, Esq. Russel-Street, Covent Garden.
Kaye Mrs. Saville-Row.
Kearton Mrs. Highgate.
Kedington Rev. Robert. Rougham-Hall, Suffolk.
Keeling John Esq. Tottenham.
Kelham Miss.
Kemble Thomas, Esq.
Kemp Richard, Esq.

Kendall

SUBSCRIBERS NAMES. xxiii

Kendall Edward, Efq. Llangaddock.
Kennett Mrs. Great Marlborough-Street.
Kent Mr. Mark-Lane.
Kent Mrs. ditto.
Kerrich Rev. ———. Magdalen College Cambridge
Kettilby Rev. Dr. Rector of St. Bartholomew the Great.
King Captain. America-Square.
King Mrs. ———. John-Street, Bedford-Row.
Kinlefide Rev. William.
Kirkman Mrs. Sarum. 2 copies.
Knapp William Jerome, Efq. Harpur-Street, Red Lion-Square.
Knill Mr. John. Grays-Inn Square.
Knottesford Rev. Francis Fortifcue. Tottenham.
Knowlys Mr. Edmonton.
Knowlys Mrs. ditto.
Knowlys Newman, Efq. Temple.
Knowlys Mr. I. Stockwell.
Kymer John, Efq.


L.

London the Right Rev. the Lord Bifhop of. 5 copies.
Litchfield and Coventry the Hon. and Rt. Rev. the Lord Bifhop of. 2 copies.
Lake Sir James Winter, Bart. Edmonton.
Lake Lady. ditto.
Lady A.
Lady A. Edmonton.

Lambert

## SUBSCRIBERS NAMES.

Lambert Mr. Daniel. St. Martin's Lane, Cannon-Street.
Lambert Mifs. Lamb's-Conduit-Street.
Lancafter Thomas, Efq. Old-Jewry.
Landon William Efq. Chefhunt.
Landon Rev. Charles. Fellow of Sidney Coll. Camb.
Landon Mifs. Chefhunt.
Landon Mr. John. ditto.
Lane George Efq. Loman's Pond.
Lang Robert, Efq. Finfbury-Square.
Langley Mrs. Glocefter-Street, Queen-Square.
Langton Mr. Zechariah. Bread-Street.
Laprimaudaye Rev. Charles. Auftin-Friars.
Latham Mrs. Eltham.
Law Rev. Dr. Archdeacon of Rochefter.
Law Edward, Efq. Bloomfbury-Square.
Law Mrs.
Lawford Mr. Samuel. Peckham.
Lawford Mr. Thomas. Gracechurch-Street.
Lawman Major.
Lawrence Mr. Richard. Camberwell.
Lawrence Mrs.
Lawrie P. Efq. Lawrence-Pountney Hill.
Lawrie Robert Efq. Lincoln.
Lawrie Mr. I. D. City-Chambers.
Lawfon Rev. George. M. A. Trinity College, Camb.
Lawton Mr.
Lax Rev. Mr. Profeffor Trinity Coll. Cam. 10 copies.
Leachman Mrs. —— Hoddefdon, Herts.
Lee R. Efq. Highbury-Place.
Lee R. Jun. Efq. Old-Broad-Street.

Lee

Lee William, Esq.
Lee Mrs.
Lee Mr. Launcelot. Fellow of New-College, Oxford.
Lee George, Esq. Ilford.
Lee James, Esq.
Leeds Joseph, Esq. 2 copies.
Legrew Mr. Edmonton.
Legrew Rev. James. M. A. St. John's, Cambridge.
Leigh Mrs. Elizabeth.
Leir Rev. Paul. Ditchet.
Leitch Lewis, Esq. Lambeth-Terrace.
Leitch Capt. Alexander. ditto.
Lenthal Mrs. ——. Priory, Burford.
Lermitte Mr. Thomas. Aldgate.
Le Souef Mr. John. Spital-Square.
L'Estrange Mrs. Norwich.
Lettsom Dr. Grove-Hill, Camberwell. 5 copies.
Lewis Rev. David.
Lewis Thomas, Esq. Palmer's-Green.
Leyborne Mrs. Westwell-House, Burford.
Lisle Mrs. Bath. 3 copies.
Livie Robert, Esq. Broad-Street Buildings.
Lloyd Rev. John. LL. B. Rector of St. Dunstan's, East.
Lloyd Mrs. ——. Chichester.
Lloyd Miss.
Longe Rev. Dr. Rector of Chelsfield, Kent.
Lubbock John, Esq. Mansion-House-Street.
Lyde Mrs. Bath.
Lynes Mrs. Clapton.
Lyon Lawrence, Esq.

Lysons

Lysons Daniel, M. D. Bath.
Lysons Rev. Daniel. Putney.
Lysons Mrs. Sarah. Hempstead, Glocester.

## M.

Middleton Lady Viscountess.
Martin Lady Dowager.
Martin Sir Henry, Bart. Weymouth-Street.
Martin Lady. 4 copies.
Mac' George ———, Esq. Bond-Street.
Mac' George Mrs.
Machay Mr. Turnham-Green.
Mackenzie James, Esq. New-Broad-Street.
Madden James, Esq. Fulham.
Maddison John, Esq. Charing-Cross.
Makay Eric, Esq. Basinghall-Street.
Malden James, Esq. Putney.
Malden Jonas, Esq.
Mallard Richard, Esq.
Malliet Mrs. Gerrard-Street.
Mann Rev. Thomas.
Manning Mrs. Totteridge.
Marlow Rev. Dr. President of St. John's, Oxford.
Marratt Webb, Esq.
Marriott Rev. R.
Martin Mrs. ———. White-Knights.
Mascall Miss. Mansfield-Street, Goodman's-Fields.
Mason Edward, Esq. Stewart-Street, Spital-Fields.

Masters

## SUBSCRIBERS NAMES.

Masters Mr. Edmonton.
Matthews James, Esq. Jesus-College, Oxford.
Maule Rev. John. Royal-Hospital, Greenwich.
Mayaffre Miss. Percy-Street.
Mayo Rev. Dr. Rector of St. George's, East.
Mayo Mrs.
Mayo Rev. Mr. Professor, Fellow of St. John's, Oxford.
Mayo Miss.
Mayo Miss Jane.
Mayo Mr. Charles. Nicholas-Lane, Lombard-Street.
Meakham Rev. W. B. Bath.
Mellish William, Esq. M. P. and Family, Bishopsgate-Street. 19 copies.
Mellish Peter, Esq.
Mello Arn. Esq. Clapham.
Mello Abraham, Esq. Highbury.
Menet Francis Esq. Southgate.
Merle Mr. Little-Britain.
Merrick Mr.
Merrick Mrs.
Mesman Daniel Esq. Spital-Square.
Mesman Mrs.
Metcalf Joseph, Esq. Clapham.
Methold Rev. Thomas. Rector of Stoneham, Suffolk.
Meyrick Mrs. Ann. Great George-Street, Westminster.
Middleton Robert Esq. Caroline-Street, Bedford-Square.
Middleton Mrs. Town-Hill, Hants.
Miller Rev. Combe. Dean of Chichester.
Milligan Richard, Esq.
Mills Thomas, Esq. Grove-House, Streatham. 50 copies.

## SUBSCRIBERS NAMES.

Mills Mrs.
Minshull Edward Esq. Milbank Street, Westminster.
Mitchell David, Esq.
Mitchell Mrs. Wimpole-Street, Cavendish-Square.
Mocher Mrs. Enfield.
Mohringk Thomas George Esq. Tottenham.
Monck Mr. Bath.
Monk Miss. Edmonton.
Monk Miss E.
Monkland Mr. Bath.
Monkland Mrs. ditto.
Monoux Rev. P. Rector of Sandy.
Moore Rev. Thomas. Rector of North-Cray.
Moore Rev. Charles. Vicar of Boughton-Blean, Kent.
Moore Frank, Esq. North Church, Herts.
Moore John, Esq. Bath.
Morres ——, Esq.
Morris Rev. T. R. Bath.
Morrison General. Hammersmith.
Morrison Mrs.           ditto.
Morrison Miss.          ditto.
Morton Mrs. Lower-Grosvenor-Street.
Moss Mrs. near Southampton.
Mourier I. Esq. Finsbury-Square.
Murrison Mrs. Bath.
Musgrave Rev. William, LL.D. Fellow of St. John's, Oxford. 5 copies.
Myddleton William, Esq.
Myers Rev. John. Witley, near Godalmin.

## N.

Northampton Countefs Dowager of. Richmond.
Neave Sir Richard, Bart.
Neave Lady.
Nanfon Mr. William. Bridge-Street, Black-Friars.
Nafh ———, Efq.
Naffau ———, Efq. Oporto. 2 copies.
Neale John, Efq.
Nepean Evean, Efq. Secretary ro the Admiralty.
Newbon Rev. Richard. Vicar of Enfield.
Newland Abraham, Efq. Bank. 5 copies.
Newman Mifs. Great-Quebec Street, Portman-Square.
Newnbey ———, Efq.
Newton Rev. Mr. Enfield.
Nichols Mr. Deputy.
Nicholl George, Efq.
Nixon John, Efq. Cateaton-Street. 3 copies.
Noble Robert, Efq.
Norris Mr.
North ———, Efq.
North Mrs. New-Bridge-Street, Black-Friars.
North Rev. ———. Afhdon.
Northage Mr. William.
Nunn William, Efq. Tooting.
Nutt Jofeph, Efq. Broad-Street.

## O.

Orford Earl of.
Oxford the Right Rev. the Lord Bishop of.
Ongley Lord. Old-Warden, Bigglefwade.
Ongley Hon. S.　　　　　ditto.
Ogle George, Efq.
Ogle Rev. George.
Oldham James, Efq. Edmonton. 2 copies.
Olier Mrs. Bloomfbury-Square
Olivier Rev. ———. Rector of Clifton, Bedfordfhire.
Olivier Mrs. Bigglefwade.
Ommanney Edward, Efq. Bloomfbury-Square.
Ommanney Mrs.
Ord Colonel. 2 copies.
Ord Mrs.
Owen Mrs. Smythe.
Owen Dr. Llwyndu. Merionethfhire.
Owen Rev. G. Rector of Llanenddwyn. ditto.

## P.

Peachey Lady. Wimpole-Street.
Pufey Hon. Philip. Pufey-houfe, Berks. 2 copies.
Page ———, Efq. Bath.
Page ———, Efq. Oporto.
Palmer Thomas, Efq. Carfhalton. 10 copies.
Palmer Mrs.
Palmer Mr. Archdale.
　　　　　　　　　　　　　　Palmer

## SUBSCRIBERS NAMES.

Palmer Mr. William.
Palmer Rev. Thomas, M. A. St. John's, Oxford.
Palmer William, Esq. Nasing.
Palmer I. F. Esq. Worcester-College, Oxford.
Palmer Mrs. ———. Richmond.
Pardon John, Esq. Southwark.
Paris Mrs. Wanstead.
Parker Samuel, Esq. South-Lambeth.
Parker ———, Esq.
Parker Mr. James. Southgate.
Parkinson Dr. Cambridge.
Parkinson Mrs.
Parnell Mr. Hugh. Spitalfields.
Paroissien Rev. ———. Hackney.
Parry Rev. ———. Warden of Ruthyn.
Parry Rev. ———. Rector of Llanabar.
Parry ———, Esq.
Parry Mr.
Parsons Rev. ———. Fellow of Baliol College, Oxford.
Pasley John, Esq. Coneyhatch.
Paterson G. Esq. Clapton.
Paterson John, Esq. John-Street, Minories.
Patten Jonathan, Esq. John-Street, Adelphi.
Paulham Mrs.
Peacock Mr. William. Salisbury-Court, Fleet-Street.
Pearse Rev. ———. Rector of Nutfield, Oxfordshire.
Pearson Wilson, Esq. Bridekirk, Cumberland.
Peatlett William, Esq.
Peck Mrs. Bath.
Peck Miss. ditto.

Pemberton

## SUBSCRIBERS NAMES.

Pemberton Rev. Jeremiah. Cambridge.
Penchback William, Efq.
Penn Mr. Stoke-Newington.
Penoyer, T. S. Efq.
Pepper John, Efq.
Perrott John, Efq.
Perry ———, Efq. Oporto. 2 copies.
Peters George, Efq. Old Bethlem.
Petley Mrs. Riverhead.
Phillips Mr. James. Tower-Street.
Phyn James, Efq. Mark-Lane. 5 copies.
Pickard Mifs. Colchefter.
Pindar George, Efq. Charing-Crofs.
Pinder Rev. ———.
Pingo Mifs. Edmonton.
Pitt Rev. L. K.
Pitt Mrs. Mortlake.
Platel James, Efq. Lincoln's-Inn.
Platt Rev. Charles. Fellow of Queen's, Cambridge.
Platt John, Efq. Broad-Street.
Platt Mrs. Ann.      ditto.      2 copies.
Plummer ———, Efq. Peckham.
Polhill Robert, Efq. Parliament-Street.
Pope Rev. ———. Fellow of St. John's, Oxford.
Pope Mrs. ———.
Pope Mifs. Great Queen-Street.
Poftlethwaite Rev. Dr. Mafter of Trinity, Camb.
Potter Mr. Charing-Crofs.
Powell Thomas, Efq. Tottenham. 10 copies.
Powell Mrs.          ditto.       10 copies

Powell

Powell James, Esq. Clapton.
Powell Miss. Homerton.
Powell F. Clark, Esq. ditto.
Powell David, jun. Esq. ditto.
Powell Walter, Esq. Tooting.
Powell ——, Esq. Cheam.
Prager Mr.
Pratt Rev. ——. Vicar of Orpington.
Prest Mr. William. Lewisham.
Prestwidge Mr. John. Mincing-Lane.
Price Rev. Dr. Prebendary of Durham.
Price William, Esq. Vice-Chamberlain to the Queen.
Prince Mr. Joseph. Borough.
Proffer Rev. Dr. ——. 2 copies.
Provis William, Esq. Bath. 5 copies.
Provis Mrs. 2 copies.
Pryse Rev. John. Trawsfynydd.
Pugh Rev. H. Rector of Hutton, Essex.
Pugh, D. H. Esq.
Pugh Mrs. Garthmaelan, North Wales.
Pugh Howel, Esq. Dolgelly.
Pybus Charles Small, Esq. M. P.

### R.

Rochester the Right. Rev. the Lord. Bishop of. 2 copies.
Rochester the Rev. the Dean and Chapter of.
Rawlinson Sir Walter.
Raikes Charles, Esq. 2 copies.

Raikes William, Esq.
Raikes Mrs. William.
Raikes Thomas, Esq.
Raikes Mrs. Thomas.
Raikes W. M. Esq.
Raikes I. M. Esq.
Ranking Mr. G. Hampstead.
Rasch Mr. John-Peter. Tokenhouse-Yard.
Rayer William, Esq.
Read William, Esq. Peckham.
Readshaw Rev. Caleb. Richmond, Yorkshire.
Reed. Gilfred Lawson, Esq. Hackney.
Reed Wilford, Esq. Lower-Thames-Street.
Reeves Mrs. Ipswich.
Reid Andrew, Esq.
Reid Mr. T. Coleman-Street-Buildings.
Relph Mrs. Mark-Lane.
Revet Rev. Thomas. Rector of Marsfield, Sussex.
Reynolds Mrs. Clophill.
Rhodes Miss. Hoxton.
Rhudde Rev. Dr. Rector of East-Bergholt, Suff. 10 cop.
Richardley John, Esq. Walworth.
Richards Miss. Bath.
Richards Rev. ———. Fellow of Oriel College, Oxford.
Richardson Rev. ———. Benet College, Cambridge.
Richardson R. Esq.
Richardson Thomas, Esq.
Rigg Miss. Bristol.
Rivington Mr. Charles. St. Paul's Church-Yard.
Roberts Rev. ———. Archdeacon of Merioneth.

## SUBSCRIBERS NAMES.

Roberts Rev. Dr. High-Master of St. Paul's School,
Roberts Miss. East-Bergholt.
Roberts Miss. Edmonton. 2 copies.
Roberts Thomas, Esq. Lambs-Conduit-Street.
Robinson Commodore.
Robinson Rev. John. M.A. Rector of Crickfea, Essex
Robinson Mrs. Edmonton.
Robinson Miss. ditto.
Rodbard Samuel, Esq. Evercreech. 5 copies.
Roebuck John, Esq.
Rogens John, Esq. Yarlington-Lodge.
Rogers Mr. Robert. Edmonton.
Rondeau Mr. James.
Roper John, Esq. Mansel-Street.
Rose Rev. John. Rector of St. Martin Outwitch.
Rose George, Esq. Stratford.
Ross Mrs. Norwich.
Rouse Rev. Ezekiel. Vicar of Clophill and Polluxhill Bedfordshire.
Row ——, Esq. Tottenham-Green.
Rowlett W. Esq. St. Helens.
Royd Mrs. Putney-Hill.
Rucker I. A. Esq. Wandsworth. 2 copies.
Rucker Daniel Henry, Esq.
Rumball Mr. Thomas. Edmonton.
Ryves Rev. Henry P. Elsted. 2 copies.
Ryves Mrs.
Ryves Miss.
Ryves, G. T. Esq.

S. Stafford

## SUBSCRIBERS NAMES.

### S.

Stafford Countefs of.
Salifbury the Rt. Rev. the Lord Bifhop of.
Seymour Lord William.     Scend. Wilts.
Seymour Hon. and Rev. Edward. ditto.
Salmon Mrs. Edmonton.
Salmon Mifs. ditto.
Salt Mifs. Tottenham.
Santen, A. A. Efq. Enfield.
Saunders Mr. Thomas, Haydon-Square,
Schneider Henry John, Efq. Southgate.
Schrieber, I. C. Efq. Denmark-Hill.
Schroder Robert, Efq.
Scott Mrs, Gower-Street.
Scott Mr.
Scott Mrs.
Scott Mrs. S.
Scott John, Efq.
Scott Mr. Samuel,
Scott James, Efq. Hammerfmith.
Sellon John Baker, Efq. Lincoln's-Inn.
Sergrove Rev. Dr. late Mafter of Pembroke College, Oxford. 2 copies.
Sewell Mr. John. Cornhill.
Seymour Mrs. Camberwell.
Shard Mifs Sophia. Peckham.
Sharp, Rev. I. Clapham.
Shaw James, Efq. America-Square.

Shawe

Shawe William Cunliffe, Esq. Southgate.
Shepherd George, Esq. High-Grove.
Shepherd Edward, Esq. Peckham.
Sheppard, Rev. Samuel Philip. Wickham, Kent.
Sheppard Mrs. Denham.
Sheppard Miss. Serle-Street. 5 copies.
Shirby Mr. Thomas.
Shrimpton Joseph, Esq. Bedford-Square.
Sibley William George, Esq. Queen-Square.
Sibley George, Esq. Crescent, Minories.
Sikes Thomas, Esq. Hackney.
Silvester John, Esq. Common-Sergeant, Chancery-Lane.
Simion Edward, Esq. Bishopsgate-Street.
Simon Mrs. Morton, Surry. 10 copies.
Sissmore Rev. H. Fellow of New-College, Oxford.
Skirrow, Mr. William. Borough.
Skottow ——, Esq.
Slade Mr. Thomas. Bartholomew-Close.
Slade Mr. Daniel. Borough.
Slade Mrs. Bath.
Smith Rev. T. I.
Smith Mrs. Drummond. Piccadilly.
Smith Isaac, Esq. Palmers-Green.
Smith Rev. Richard. M. A. Fellow of Trinity-College, Cambridge.
Smith Henry, Esq. Grove-Hill. 2 copies.
Smith ——, Esq. Champion-Hill, Surry.
Smith John, Esq. Finsbury-Square.
Smiton Mr. William.
Smyth Rev. L. Vicar of Southill.

Smyth,

Smyth Rev. John. Christ-Church College, Oxford.
Smyth Miss. Southill.
Smyth Mr. Alexander. Mark-Lane.
Snell Mrs. Edmonton.
Snell John, Esq. ditto.
Sowerby Mr. Fenchurch-Street.
Sparrow Rev. ———.
Spence Luke, Esq. Malling, Sussex.
Spence Mr. Robert. Borough.
Spitta C. L. Esq. Peckham.
Spong Mr. John. St. Margarets-Hill.
Spragg Rev. Harvey. Welbeck-Street.
Spranger John, Esq. Lincoln's Inn.
Stanback John, Esq. Lambeth-Terrace.
Stanley ———, Esq. Lime-Street.
Stedman Miss. Ayling. near Midhurst.
Steers Isaac, Esq. Temple. 5 copies.
Stephani Mrs. Clement's Lane.
Stephenson, Mrs. John. Queen-Square.
Stephenson ——— and Co. ———. 6 copies.
Stert Richard, Esq. Southgate.
Stevens Francis, Esq. Commissioner of the Victualling.
Stevens, R. I. S. Lambeth-Walk.
Stevens William, Esq. Broad-Street. 5 copies.
Stevenson Rowland, Esq.
Stevenson Mr. I. Queen-Square.
Stevenson Mrs.         ditto. 2 copies.
Stevenson ———, Esq. Grace-Church-Street.
Stinton Rev. Dr. Rector of Exeter College, Oxford.
Stirling William, Esq. Wantage.
          Stockwell

Stockwell John, Esq. Crutched-Friars.
Stowe Rev. Nevil.
Stowe Mrs.
Stringer Miles, Esq. Peckham.
Suft ——, Esq.
Sutton Mrs. 2 copies.
Swann ——, Esq. Oporto. 2 copies.
Sweet David, Esq. Gittisham, Devon.
Swinney Mr. Pall-Mall.
Symonds Rev. I. Hackney.

T.

Turner Rev. Dr. Dean of Norwich.
Taddy Christopher, Esq.
Tanner Mrs.
Tapenden —, Esq. Foster-Lane, Cheapside.
Tarbutt George, Esq. Gould-Square, Cooper's-Row.
Tash William, Esq. Broomfield-House.
Tash Mrs.
Tatem George, Esq. Hart-Street, Bloomsbury.
Tatem Mrs. Edmonton. 2 copies.
Tatlock Mr. James. Coleman-Street.
Taylor Rev. Henry. Tottenham-Court-Road.
Taylor Robert, Esq. Crutched-Friars.
Taylor Mrs. ditto.
Taylor Mrs. Edmonton.
Taylor Mr. Wager.
Teissier Stephen, Esq.

Tempest

Tempeft Mrs. Eaft-Barnet.
Temple R. G. Efq. Roehampton.
Tennant I. Efq.
Terrett Mrs. Hackney.
Tefhmaker Mrs. Winchmore-Hill.
Tefhmaker Mifs.   ditto.
T. F.
Thacrah John, Efq. Tooley-Street.
Theed John, Efq.
Theed Thomas, Efq. Edmonton.
Theobalds Mrs. Kew.
Thomas Rev. M. Sutton-Lodge.
Thomas Mrs. M. Camberwell.
Thomas Mrs. N.
Thomas Rev. G. A. Rector of Woolwich, Kent.
Thomas Rice, Efq. Norfolk-Street.
Thomas Mrs. Watergate-Houfe, Suffex.
Thompfon Mrs. Finfbury-Square.
Thwaites Mrs. Highbury-Terrace.
Till Mr. Richard. London-Bridge.
Timperon Jofeph, Efq.
Timfon, W. Efq. Moor-Park.
Topham John, Efq.
Torriano Major. Kenfington-Square. 3 copies.
Torriano Mrs. fenior.
Torriano Mrs. I. S.
Totton Rev. W. I. Denham.
Totton Mifs.
Totton Stevens, Efq. Spital-Square. 2 copies.
Totton Mrs.   ditto.

Totton

# SUBSCRIBERS NAMES.

Totton Stevens Dineley, Efq. Madras.
Tottons Mifs. Lamb's-Conduit-Street.
Toulmin Rev. Dr. Taunton, Somerfetfhire.
Townley Mifs. Weymouth.
Townfend Henry Hare, Efq.
Townfend Mrs.
Towry Mrs. Ormond-Street.
Travers John, Efq. Crutched Friars.
Travers Mrs.          ditto.
Travers Mifs.          ditto.
Travers Mifs C.     ditto.
Trecothick James, Efq. Addington, Surry.
Trotter William, Efq.
Tunftall Mr.
Turner Mrs. Putney.
Turner Mifs. Southampton-Street, Bloomfbury.
Tutt Rev. Francis. Rector of Shering, Effex.
Tyers James, Efq.

## U.

Uphill Rev. George. Lamiet.
Uvedale Admiral. Bofmere, Suffolk.
Uvedale Mrs.         ditto.
Uvedale Rev. Dr. Rector of Langton, Lincolnfhire.

Vaillant

## V.

Vaillant Paul, Efq. Pall-Mall.
Vaillant Rev. Philip. ditto.
Vaillant John, Efq. Temple.
Vardon Thomas, Efq. Gracechurch-Street.
Vere James, Efq.
Vere Peter, Efq.
Vetch Mrs.
Veyfie Rev. ———. Fellow of Oriel College, Oxford

## W.

Winchefter the Hon. and Rt. Rev. the Ld. Bp. of. 2 cop.
Wombwell Lady.
Wakeman Thomas, Efq. St. Mildred's Court.
Wale Major.
Wale Mifs.
Walker Ifaac, Efq. Arno's Grove. 2 copies.
Wall Martin, M. D. Chymical-Profeffor. Oxford.
Walfby Rev. Dr. Prebendary of Canterbury.
Walter Rev. ———. Crayford.
Warburton Rev. William, M. A.
Ward Mr. Benjamin.
Ward Mr. John. Ludgate-Hill.
Ward Mifs.
Waring Mrs. Brompton. 2 copies.
Warner Mr. John. Edmonton.

Warren

# SUBSCRIBERS NAMES.

Warren Rev. Dawson. Vicar of Edmonton. 5 copies.
Warren Mrs. Dawson,
Warren Charles, Esq.
Warren Mrs.
Washam Mrs. S.
Washbourne Mrs. Edmonton. 3 copies.
Wathen Miss C.
Watkins Mrs. Daventry.
Watkins Miss. ditto.
Watson Rev. John.
Watson John, Esq.
Watson Joshua, Esq.
Way Mrs. Richmond.
Webb Mrs. ditto. 2 copies.
Webster Rev. Dr. Bath.
Webster Rev. Richard. F*** *** of St. John's Coll. Oxf.
Webster Rev. W. Rector of Mepershall.
Weightman Mr.
Welles Rev. Richard. University College, Oxford
Wells Mr. Bigglesdwade.
Wetherell Rev. Dr. Master of University Coll. Oxford.
Wetherell Rev. Robert. Fellow of New College, Oxf.
Whitbread Samuel, Esq.
White Mrs. Soho-Square.
White James, Esq. Chancery-Lane.
White S. Esq. Clapham.
Whitehead Mr. Basinghall-Street.
Whitehead Miss. Edmonton.
Whitelock Mrs.
Whitelock Miss.

Whitelock

SUBSCRIBERS NAMES.

Whitelock Rev. R. H. Farthinggoe, Northamptonshire.
Whitfield Mr. John. St. Thomas's Hospital.
Whitfield Rev. Thomas. Fellow of St. John's Coll. Ox.
Whitmarsh Henry, Esq.
Whitmore John, Esq. Old Jewry.
Whittingstall Mrs. Hoddesdon. 5 copies.
Wickham Rev. Provis.
Wickham Mrs.
Wickham John, Esq. New-College, Oxford. 5 copies.
Wickham Mrs. ———. Wells.
Wigston John, Esq. Trent-Park. 3 copies.
Wigston Mrs.          ditto.      2 copies.
Wigzell Thomas, Esq.
Wilcox Mrs. Hoddesdon.
Wilcox Mr.       ditto.
Wilcox Mr. Edmond. ditto.
Wilcox Rev. ———. Loughborough.
Wildman Mrs. Twickenham.
Wilkinson Mrs.
Wilkinson Miss.
Wilkinson Jacob, Esq.
Wilkinson Mrs. Twickenham.
Wilkinson, Miss Nancy. ditto.
Willes John, Esq. Dulwich.
Willey William, Esq. Edmonton.
Williams Mrs. Crescent, Bath.
Williams Capt.
Williamson Mrs. Edmonton.
Williamson Rev. G. Rector of Campton.
Willis, Rev. John Law. Pickwith.

Willis,

## SUBSCRIBERS NAMES.

Willis Mr. Wellingboro', Northamptonshire.
Wilmot Francis, Esq. St. John's College, Oxford.
Wilson, Mr. Joseph. Cannon-Street.
Wilson Robert, Esq. Prescott-Street.
Winbolt Rev. Thomas. M. A. Minister of Southgate Chapel.
Winbolt James, Esq. New-Basinghall-Street.
Winder Mrs. Putney.
Winterbottom S. Esq.
Wintle Rev. ———. Rector of Brightwell, Berks.
Wintle Rev. ———. Fellow of Pembroke College, Oxford.
Winwood, Mr. James. Edmonton.
Wise Rev. Dr. Archdeacon of Coventry.
Withers John, Esq. Dover Place.
Wolff George, Esq. Danish Consul.
Wood Edmond, Esq. near Chichester. 5 copies.
Wood Mr. John. Fox-Ordinary-Court.
Wood Mrs.
Woodbridge John, Esq.
Woodbridge James, Esq.
Woodcock Mrs. Enfield. 3 copies.
Woodcock Miss, S. ditto.
Woodcock Capt.
Woodford Rev. T. Ansford.
Woodhouse James, Esq.
Wooding Mr. Richard. Bouvine-Street, Fleet-Street.
Woodyear ———, Esq.
Woolrych Mrs. Southgate.
Worsfold Mrs. Edmonton. 3 copies.
Worsley Rev. Ralph. M. A.
Worth Mr. John.

Worthington

Worthington Samuel, Efq. Jeffery's-Square, St. Mary Axe.
Wortledge Robert, Efq. Great St. Helens.
Wrench Mrs. Camberwell.
Wright Mr. Alderman.
Wright Rev. ———. Duke-Street, Manchefter-Square.
Wright Samuel, Efq.
Wrighte Rev. William. M. A.
Wroughton Mrs. Eaft-Barnet.
Wyatt Mrs. Foard-Houfe, Devizes.
Wynne Dr. William. Lincolns-Inn Fields. 2 copies.

## X.

X. X. ———. 5 copies.

## Y.

York His Grace the Archbifhop of. 10 copies.
Yates Lady.
York Major.
York Mifs.
Young Brown, Efq.
Younge Rev. George. South-Malling, Effex.

### ADDITION.

Butts Rev. William. Rector of Glemsford, Suffolk.

www.ingramcontent.com/pod-product-compliance
Lightning Source LLC
Chambersburg PA
CBHW020104020526
44112CB00033B/815